'ARAB

MUSLIM ADMINISTRATION

(622 – 1258)

S. M. IMAMUDDIN

D.Phil. (Calcutta), D.Phil. & Litt. (Madrid)
Professor of Islamic History and Culture
University of Dacca

KITAB BHAVAN
New Delhi-1 10002

Published by
Nusrat Ali Nasri for Kitab Bhavan
1214, Kalan Mahal, Darya Ganj, New Delhi-110 002

Printed at
ADITYA OFFSET PRESS
2330, Kucha chellan, Daryaganj, New Delhi-110002

PREFACE

Having written *the Political history of the Muslims* (from Prophet Muḥammad to the 'Abbāsids) in two volumes and *the Political history of Muslim Spain* (711–1492), it was deemed necessary to compile a work on Administration under the Arabs giving a continuous history of their administration at Madīnah, Damascus, Baghdād, Cordova and Cairo at different pericds. It seeks to give a vivid picture of the administrative set-up of the governments, civil and military, *albiet* brief and short. While dealing with the institutions of administration their historical growth and development have been kept in view throughout the discussion and their assessment has been made in the *Resume*.

Of the Arabic sources in original or translation mainly the works of Balādhurī, Tabarī, Mas'ūdī, Abū Yūsuf, Qudāmah, Ibn Qutaybah, al-Isfahānī, al-Māwardi, Ibn 'Idhārī, Ibn al-Khatīb, Ibn Bassām, Maqqarī, Maqrīzī, Ibn Tiqtaqah, al-Qalqashandī, Jahshiyārī, Suyūtī, al-Nadīm, Ibn Khaldūn and others have been consulted and depended upon. Critical notices of some of them have been appended here in the Introduction serving as an index to the nature of materials utilised in giving shape to this short work on '*Arab administration* much needed by regular students and interested laymen. The author will feel his labour amply rewarded if their purpose is served.

Among the modern works, the books of Mez, Von Kremer, Levy, Hitti, Levi-Provencal, Vatikiotis, Gaston Wiet, Mu'īn al-Dīn Nadvī, Scott, Montgomery Watt, Zāhid 'Alī, Jurjī Zaydān, Khudā Bakhsh, Husainī and of the present author himself have been of great help in preparing the text of this work. The author acknowledges the medieval as well as modern writers mentioned above as his authorities and, in case of a successful presentation of the subject. he feels that credit goes mainly to those pioneers in the field alone on the fruits of whose researches the present writer has largely depended. The present work is intended to be a companion volume of '*the Political History of the Muslims from Prophet Muhammad to the 'Abbasids*' and also of the author's other works on *Muslim Spain.*

The author is conscious of his shortcomings in the plan of this book and also its execution and others to which his attention may be drawn by learned crit cs on reviewing this work. Because of non-availability and short supply of diacritical signs '*irab* (accent marks) could not be put properly in some cases giving in-complete accent.

University of Dacca
September, 1975 S. M. IMAMUDDIN

CONTENTS

Maps

CHAPTER I

SOURCES

Learning and literature received great impetus, private and official, throughout the Muslim countries particularly from the 9th to the 13th centuries producing a large number of literature on various subjects at different stages of the history. Scholars wrote widely on history and geography and on various aspects of administration. Unfortunately many of these source books are lost. Materials for writing an administrative history of the Muslim 'Arabs are, however, scattered throughout the Arabic literature dealing mainly with history, geography, biographies, judicial and police affairs, *hisbah* etc. Of the sources extant, some major works of the following authors are analysed here critically leaving out others already discussed elsewhere.

Abū Yūsuf (d.*ca.* 789) the most illustrious pupil of Imām Abū Hanīfah was appointed the first Qādī al-Qudat of the 'Abbasid court by al-Mahdī. He served under him and his sons Hādī and al-Hārūn. The chief view of the teachings imparted by Abū Hanīfah to his disciples have been preserved by Abū Yūsuf in his *Kitab al-Kharaj*, a book written in answer to certain questions put by the Khalīfah Hārūn al-Rashīd. He advised Hārūn to appoint separate '*Amils*' to collect *zakat* and held that the *zakat* collected from each town should be distributed in that very town and the revenue from the *ṣadaqat* (charities) of the Muslims should not be mixed up with that collected from the *Kharaj*. According to him the forests (*al-ajam*), marshes (*al-bata'ih*) and waste-lands (*al-mawat*) reclaimed by Muslims but without watering from the *Kharaj* streams (*Anharu'l-Kharaj*) were included in the '*Ushrī* lands. He held that the Christians of Banu Taghlib and Najrān were exempt from the payment of *jizyah* but in lieu of this the Banū Taghlib Christians had to pay double the *zakat*. Declaring 'Umar's fixation of the rates of taxes injurious to the interest of the public treasury, Abū Yūsuf issued a legal decree authorising the Khalīfah to change the rates fixed by 'Umar. Because of the contractor's extortions Abū Yūsuf condemned *al-taqbīl* system the buying and selling of tax-farms done under the early Abbasids unless *al-muqabbil* (contractor) was just and such transaction was approved by the village people. Abū Yūsuf informs that non-Muslim traders of Manbij were the first to be allowed to trade in Muslim countries on paying tithes (*al-'ushūr*) as tax, although not mentioned in the *Qura'n* but was first imposed by 'Umar I. Abū Yūsuf informs us that during the time of the Prohpet, of the soldiers' share in the booty three shares went to the horsemen, two for maintaining horses and one for maintaining themselves while the infantry received only one-third of the share of the horseman. Abū Yūsuf denounced the ill-treatment of non-Muslim tax-payers because it was against Islamic principles. For the protection of the tax-payers from the oppression of the tax-collectors Abū Yūsuf suggested for maintenance of a strong espionage system.

There is another work on *al-Kharaj* by Qudāmah a Christian by birth. He accepted Islām and served the Abbasids in the early years of the 10th century as revenue accountant in the central government of Baghdād and wrote the *Kitab al-Kharaj* soon after 928 discussing the division of the Caliphate under Mu'taṣim (833-42) into provinces, the digging of Nahr al-Silah in Wāsit by al-Mahdi (775-78), the construction of metalled road from al-Qadisiyah to Zubala by Mahdī, the collection of taxes from the districts and the organisation of postal service in the provincial and district towns. From the balance sheet prepared most probably, under Mu'taṣim by Qudāmah it appears that income from the Sawād in Lower 'Irāq both in cash and kind was equivalent to 130,200,000 dirhams, from Egypt 37,500,000, from Khurāsān 37,000,000, from Syria and Palestine 15,860,000 and from all over the empire in total 388,291, 350 dirhams which figures, however, do not tally with the total of the figures given by him in de ails itemwise.

Ibn Qutaybah (d. 889 A. D.) whose family flourished at Marv, properly called Muḥammad ibn Muslim, held the office of Qādī at Dināwar and lived at Baghdād towards the end of the 9th century. He is the celebrated author of a number of books of which *Kitabu'l-Ma'arif* (Book of General knowledge), '*Uyūn al-*

Akhbar (*Choice Histories*), *Ādab'l Katib* (Accomplishments of the Secretary), and *Kitabu'l Shi'r wa'l-Shu'ara'* (Book of Poetry and Poets) are extant. The *Kitab al-Ma'arif* deals with the creation, the history of the Prophets, racial divisions of mankind and genealogies of the Arabs, Prophet Muḥammad, four orthodox Caliphs, Umayyads, Abbasids down to al-Mu'tamid, biographies of Muslim statesmen, officers and governors, teachers and doctors of Islam, notable rebels and the kings of Yaman, Syria, Hira and Persia down to the Sassanid dynasty.

The *'Uyūnu'l Akhbar* is a work in ten chapters each devoted to a special theme like government, war, nobility, friendship, women etc. Ibn Qutaybah also writes elaborately about the 'Arab weapons in the *'Uyūn-al-Akhbar*. The *Ādabu'l Katib* is a manual of stylistic writings dealing with orthography, lexicography, etc.

Abū 'Abd Allāh Muḥammad b. 'Abdus al-Jahshiyārī (d. 942-3) was a learned man and skilful craftsman. He is the author of the celebrated *Kitāb al-Wuzara wa'l kuttab* (Book of Wazirs and Secretaries) which he proposed to write based on thousand tales. Basing on the Persian work *Hazar Afsanah* he selected one thousand stories of the Persians, the Greeks and other nations out of the stories related by local story tellers or read in the fabulous and story-books and arranged his materials into 480 nights, each night an entire story of about fifty pages but he died before he could complete the work. It became one of the sources of *Alf Laylah wal-Laylah* (Thousand and one Nights) which was given final shape under the Mamluk Sultans of Egypt. From the revenue chart given by al-Jahshiyārī, it is clear that there were 35 fiscal provinces under the Abbasids to which Ibn Khaldūn added one more Unit. Ja'far presided over *Dīwan al-Nazr fi'l Mazalim* and decided about thousand cases in one day under Hārūn al-Rashīd.

Abu'l-Faraj 'Alī b. al-Husayn b. al-Isfahānī (d. 967) was born at Isfahān in 284/897. By birth he was a Persian although a lined descendant of Marwān II the last Umayyad Caliph. He studied at Baghdād the centre of Islamic learning in the 10th century. Wandering about as a scholar he received patronage from Sayf al-Dawlah al-Hamadānī and the Buwayhid Wazīr Isma'il b. 'Abbād and al-Muhallabī. He died on the 14th Dhu'lijjah 356/21st November 967. Of his writings the only extant work is the *Kitab al-Āghanī*. On presenting this celebrated work on Arabic literature to Sayf al-Dawlah the author received an inadequate amount of one thousand dinars only and obtained another one-thousand dinars from Hakam II of Spain on sending its first copy to the Umayyad Caliph. Sāḥib ibn 'Abbād a Buwayhid wazīr (d.995) used to carry it always with him in journey. It is a collection of songs with the accounts of their origin and of their authors. It begins with the collection of 100 songs which were composed by Ibrāhīm al-Mawṣilī and Isma'īl b. Jāmi' and Fulayh b. al-'Awra' at the orders of the Abbasid Caliph Hārūn al-Raskīd and revised by Isḥāq b. Ibrāhīm under al-Wāthiq. Then followed other selected songs sung by Caliphs and their descendants with the detailed notices of the poets, singers and writers. Occasionally the author introduced vast quantity of historical traditions and anecdotes adding to the social and cultural importance of the work. *Al-Āghanī* records that all those who received state pensions were compelled to render military service by Hajjāj b. Yūsuf. It also informs us that the fire-balls were prepared out of sulphur, while naphtha and stones were set in the holder of the *manjaniq* and shot against forts to split its walls into pieces. Although the arrangement of the work is not systematic it is an invaluable source book for the study of Muslim civilization. It is based on the researches of great humanists which are almost perished and contains materials for writing the literary and cultural history of the period ending with the third century of the Hijrah era. "The Book of Songs" observes Ibn Khaldūn "is the Register of the Arabs. It comprised all that they have achieved in the past of excellence in every kind of poetry, history, music *et cetra.* So far as I am aware no other book can be put on a level with it in this respect. It is the final source of the student of belles-letters and leaves him nothing further to desire."[1] It was first printed in Bulaq 1284-85 and twenty years after its enlarged edition came out

1. *Muqaddama,* Beyrout, 1900, p. 554 quoted by Nicholson, *Literary History of the Arabs*, Cambridge, 1930, p. 32.

in 21 volumes from Cairo in 1905-6. A volume of biographies not contained in the Bulaq text was edited by Brunnow, R. E., Leiden, 1888.

Abu'l Faraj Muḥammad b. Isḥāq al-Nadīm Bag̲h̲dādī (d. 994 A.D.) also called *al-Warraq* (stationer or book-dealer) composed *al-Fihrist* (Index) about six years before his death in 377(987-8). His family lived at Bag̲h̲dād and like his father he was a book-seller. The author was a S̲h̲i'ī and Mu'tazili but tolerant and interested in other sects. *Al-Fihrist* is a very remarkable and valuable work in Arabic literature. It deals with the religious and literary history of Islam and the pre-Islamic period. Most of its source materials are lost. In it all books available in the Arabic language in original or translation and sold in Bag̲h̲dād Book Market have been included. It is divided into ten *maqalat* (Discourses) and each discourse is divided into two or more sections. The *Fihrist* deals with the different kinds of scripts in the introduction, then with the four revealed books, branches of literature beginning with the *Qura'n*, the *hadit̲h̲* and commentaries ending with the occult sciences. Writers have been grouped in each section in chronological order appending notices available on their lives and works. It records of an 'Irāqī bibliophile having manuscripts, parchments, Egyptian papyri and Chinese paper bearing the names of the scribes and notes of persons from five to six generations. Al-Nadim's another work *Kitab al-Awṣaf wa'l-Tas̲h̲bihat* (*Fihrist p.12*) is not extant.

Al-Māwardī who died at the age of 86 in 1058 is known for his Utopian treatise on politics *Kitab al-Aḥkam al-Sultaniyah* (*Constitutiones Politicae*). He was a S̲h̲afi'ī *faqih* (theologian) and lived at Bag̲h̲dād during the period of Buwayhid anarchy. In 429 (1037-8) when the Buwayhid Jalāl al-Dawlah asked the caliph al-Muqtadi to grant him the title of S̲h̲ahans̲h̲āh al-Māwardi objected and earned the enmity of the Buwayhid. Basing his views on theory he laid stress on the election of a caliph by a body of learned, pious and orthodox divines and on the obedience of the people to such elected caliphs. He held that only a Quray<u>sh</u> could be caliph just to estabilize the Abbasid Caliphate. According to him 'Abd al-Malik had fixed a day for hearing appeals and complaints which practice was followed by 'Umar II and later on developed into a department called *Dīwan al-Nazar fi al-Maẓalim* under the Abbasids. While d scussing justice al-Māwardi writes about two types of *qadī*: one with limited authoı ity (*Khaṣṣah*) and another with general and absolute a hority (*'ammah mutlaqah*). He also writes about two types of governorship: *imarah 'ammah* and *'imarah khassah* one with unlimited power having jurisdiction over judges and tax-collectors and the other with limited authority having no control over taxes and justice. Actually governor's power was linked up with his ability, the ability of the Caliph and distance of his province from the Central capital and the one who was ambitious enough to usurp the power of an *amīr* was called by the author *al-Amir bil-istila'*. Al-Māwardī discusses in detail the duties of the *Wali* (Governor) who heard the cases of *al-Maẓalim* or appointed an officer for that. Al-Māwardī's work on the sayings of the Prophet and his companions served as a text-book in Egyptian and Syrian schools down to the modern times.

Ibnu'l Tiqtaqa, Jalāl al-Dīn Abū Ja'far 'Alī an 'Alid by descent through al-Hasan and Ibrāhīm Tabataba of the family of Ramadan, settled at al-Hilla was born about 660/1262. He succeeded his father as a representative of the Alids in al-Hilla, Najaf and Karbalah. His wife was a Khurāsāni Persian. He journied to Marāghah in 696/1297 and Mosul in 701/1301 where he wrote *Kitabu'l Fakhrī* in 1302 and dedicated it to the Governor of Mosul, for the Mongol Sultān Ghāzān, Fakhr al-Dīn 'Isā, after whom the book was named as such. It is a delightful manual of Muslim politics and is divided into two parts, the first dealing with political treatise and the second is the summary of the dynastic history of the Muslims where each sovereign is followed by the notices of his ministers. The second part is based on Ibn al-Athīr's *Kamil al-Tawarīkh* and the lost *Annals* of Mas'ūdī. The history of ministers has been derived particularly from *Hilal al-Sabi*. It is a good introduction to Arabic literature and known for its simplicity and lucid style and for the varied interest of its contents. It informs us about the institution of *Dīwan* by 'Umar on the Persian line derived from the Persian word *dīwan* and the introduction of the system of sharing the produce of the land as suggested by al-

Mahdī's wazir 'Ubaydullah and that of *al-taqbīl* selling of farm lands to contractors under the Abbasids. It was edited by W. Ahlwardt, Gotha 1860, Hertwig Derenbourg 1895, Fr. tr. by M. Emil Amar 1910 (Archives Marocaines, t. XVI, 1910).

To ascertain and set down the true story of about three hundred years of Umayyad rule and civilization in Spain volumes would be necessary, but here only a sketch of the sources of their administration in Spain is given. Ibn 'Idhārī of Marrākush lived in the 13th century. He wrote *al-Bayan al-Mughrib fi Akhbar al-Andalus wa'l Mughrib*. Although he is not very critical in his narration of events and at times he is over-powered by a temptation to exaggerate yet valuable informations about socio-economic and administrative set up in Spain can be garnered from the pages of his work in abundance. The taxfree land of *al-Batha* known as *al-Rabd* (cemetry) in Cordova, the sale of Prince Sulayman's estate, prices of some necklaces, suits, wheat, marbles, minting of coins, public works like construction of bridges, relations of Spain with 'Irāq and other countries, relief work, flood, earthquake, destruction of cultivation by military forces, officers of inheritance, salaries, the Cordova mosque and its staff and expenditure, import of foreign articles from 'Adan and other ports are some of the numerous topics which are found in the pages of this important historical treatise.

Lisān al-Dīn ibn al-Khatīb (1313-1375) the celebrated author of *al-Ihatah fi Ta'rikh al-Gharnatah* and a contemporary of Ibn Khaldūn composed the *Kitab A'mal al-A'lam al-Thani fi Akhbar Jazirah al-Andalusiyah* between the years 775 and 776H/1372-74 A.D. Among the important materials, available in this book mention may be made of the import of necklaces and other jewellery from Baghdād in the tenth century, income and expenditure, famines, the breeding of horses and camels in Spain. the arms and ammunition factory etc

Aḥmad be Muḥammad al-Maqqarī al-Maghribī of Tilimsān (Algiers), the famous Maghribi writer of the 17th century, wrote two books the *Azhar al-Riyad fi al-Akhbar 'Iyad* (the Flowers of Meadows in the History of 'Iyād) and the *Nafh al-Tib min Ghusn al-Andalus al-Ratib wa Dhikr wazīr* Lisān al-Dīn ibn al-Khatīb

(Exhalation of Sweet smell from the Green branches of Andalus and History of the Wazir Lisān al-Dīn ibn al-Khatīb). Some of the materials of socio-economic and administrative interest which are found in the pages of the *Azhar* are the construction of the Zahrā' Palace, the import of marble and labour engaged in the construction of the Zahrā', the cost of a royal villa, the taxes collected during the time of 'Abd al-Raḥmān III al-Naṣir, metal industries of Cordova, the hiring of mules, import of furs and other valuable stuffs, the salary of a minister.

For writing *Nafh al-Tib*, Maqqarī consulted books at Tilimsān but completed the work at Damascus between the years 1628-30 A.D. during the period of his refuge in Syria. He has preserved in this valuable work many passages from other books which are lost. It is a complete history of the Muslim rule and administration in Spain although the *Nafh al-Tib* is more a piece of literature than a work of scientific history as Maqqarī seldom introduces critical or explanatory remarks of his own but always quotes his predecessors without giving a critical analysis. Credit, however, goes to Maqqarī for preserving many passages from works which are lost and for writing a chapter on Muslim administration in Spain, which is not found in complete form elsewhere in any Arabic work.

'Alī 'Abd Allāh Muḥammad bin Harīth al-Khushanī was born at Qayrawān and died in 361/971. At the instance of Prince Hakam, son of 'Abd al-Raḥmān III, he wrote the *Kitab al-Qudat bi Qurtubah* (History of the judges of Cordova). It is a social history of old Cordova and a literature concerning justice rendered by Spanish Muslims in the Middle ages. It also contains informations of Muslim culture, languages spoken in the 10th century, socio-economic life, use of dress, feasts and regulations, the qādī's subsidiary vocations as a cultivator and a manufacturer of cloth, a trustee and a banker and the depositer of public money in the court for distribution among the poor. Moreover it deals with markets and their officer *sahib al-Ahbas* or *muḥtasib*, the *hammams* (baths), despatch of letters through travellers, use of certificates and identity cards, the laws for the construction of houses and

Abu'l Hasan 'Alī b. Bassām a native of Santaren (Portugal wrote *al-Dhakhīroh fi Mahasin ahl al-jazīrah* (the Treasurer of the good qualities of the people of Spain) about 542H/1147-8. It is a sort of biographicai work of contemporary learned men and poets of Spain. It is a store house of materials relating to Hājib al-Mansūr's treasury, government stores, imports and exports, famines, prices of wheat, barley and flour and the salary of a tutor and a courtier.

Ibn 'Abdūn, the author of *al-Hisbah*, lived between the later part of the 11th century and the earlier part of the 12th in Seville. His work deals with marketing and business rules. It supplies additional informations for example women had separate markets and baths, musicians (*mulhi*) were not allowed to roam about with outpermission of the qādī because they were accompanied by people of undesireable character.

Contemporary sources not being extant one is to depend for the Fatimid administration on later sources. The Mamluk period in Egypt is rich for the production of historical works. Among the Mamluk historians were Abu'l Fidā' al-Qalqashandi, al-Maqrīzī. ibn Taghribirdī and al-Suyūtī. Abu'l-Fidā' Ismā'il b. 'Alī b. Maḥmūd b. 'Umar b. Shahanshah b. Ayyub 'Imād al-Dīn al-Ayyūbī was a prince historian and geographer. He was born in Jumāda I, 672/Nov. 1273 at Damascus where his father, a descendant of a brother of Salāh al-Dīn Ayyūbi and governor of Hamat, had taken refuge fleeing from the Mongols. In the services of his uncle Malik al-Manṣūr prince of Hamat he began his early military career. On the death of his cousin Maḥmūd II in Dhuqa'd 698/August, 1299 when the throne passed to the amir Sanqur he entered the service of Sultān al-Malik al-Nāsir. Twelve years after he was appointed governor of Hamat. In recognition of his services he was awarded the title of *Malik al-Salih* and *Malik al-Mu'aiyad* and the hereditary rank of Sultān. He died at Hamat on 23rd Muḥarram 732/27th October 1331. He patronised scholars and himself wrote books on history and geography of which *Mukhtaṣar Ta'rīkh al-Bashar* and *Taqwim al-Buldan* have come to us. The former is a historical treatise dealing with pre-Islamic h story and that of Islam up to 729/1329.

It was published in 2 volumes at Constaninople in 1286/1869-70. The later one which deals with world geography was completed in 721/1321. It was edited by Reinaud and Mac. Guckin de Slane, Paris 1840 and translated into French by Reinaud, Paris 1848.

S͟hihāb al-Dīn Abu'l 'Abbās Aḥmad b. 'Alī b. Aḥmad b. 'Abd-Allāh b. 'Ali G͟hudda briefly called Aḥmad b. 'Abd Allah and known as Aḥmad al-Qalqas͟handi (d. 10th Jumāda II 821/16th July 1418) wrote many small works and two voluminous ones. In the line of Ibn Qutaybah's *'Uyūn al-Ak͟hbar* he composed a guide to the Egyptian government officials on essays and reports entitled *Subh al-A'sh͟a fi sina'al Insh͟a*. The informations about the history and geography of Egypt and Syria contained in this book are of great importance and are rare in many cases. It deals with the military and civil administrative systems under the Fatimids and give a vivid account of the working of *Dīwan al-Taqwi'* under al-Mu'tadid (279-289/892-902). It was published in 14 volumes at Cairo in 1331-8/1913-9. His second great work is *Nihayat al-'Arab fi Ma'rifat Qaba'il 'Arab* which deals with the genealogy and history of the 'Arab tribes before Prophet Muḥammad in alphabetical order. It was composed in 812/1409. These works have been copied and abridged by later writers like Suyūtī and others in their writings.

Al-Maqrīzī is the most eminent of Mamlūk historians and known for his works *K͟hitat* and *Sulūk* on Egyptian history and antiquities. Taqi al-Din Aḥmad al-Maqrīzī (1364-1442) was born in Cairo. He was of Ba'labak ancestry. He held several high offices as a teacher and qādi in Cairo and Damascus. He is chiefly known for his writings on Egyptian topography, history and antiquities in his celebrated work *al-Mawa'iz wa'l-I'tibar fi D͟hikr al-K͟hitat wa'l-Ath͟ar* (Sermons and learning by example on an account of the new settlements and remains) published in two volumes. He is charged with plagiarism by his contemporary al-Sak͟hawi in his work *al-Tibr al-Masbuk fi D͟hayl al-Sulūk* of defect common to other writers of the line. While recording the riches of al-Mustanṣir, the richest of the Fatimid caliphs, al-Maqrīzī includes precious stones, inlaid with gold plates, ivory and ebony inkstands, ambercups, parasols with gold and silver stick phials of musk, crystal vases, steel mirrors, chess-boards with gold and silver pawns, jewelled daggers and swords, embroidered fa rics of Dabiq and Damascus, specimens of ceramic and metallic arts and Chinese glazed earthenware. According to Maqrīzī there were employed in Egypt alone 120,000 labourers annually in digging canals for irrigation and drinking purposes. He gives a vivid account of the working of the *Diwan al-Tawqi'* under al-Mu'tadid (279-289/892-902) dealing with the orders passed by Caliphs on complaints of individuals against the decisions of government officers before their circulations to provincial governors and other officials or persons concerned. It is true he is criticised for his being unconscientious and uncritical often indulging in plagiarism the characteristics of the period but he has accumulated and preserved lots of information which otherwise would have lost. He is accurate and based his information on contemporary evidence where ever possible. The author is impartial in his sta ement and his work is lucid in style.

Abu'l Maḥāsin Jamāl al-Din Yūsuf b. Taghribirdi b. 'Abd Allāh al-Zahiri al-Juwaini was born at Cairo in Shawwāl 813 February 1411. From his father side he was an 'Arab governor of Ḥalab (Aleppo) and Damascus and mother's side a Turk, a Barqūq. He was a pupil of al-Maqrīzī. He performed pilgrimage in 863/1458 and died in 874/1469 or 870/1465-66. Of his writings seven historical works are extant the most important being *al-Nujūm al-Zahirah fi mulūk Misr wa'l Qahirah* (the Brilliant stars regarding the Kings of Egypt and Cairo) which was composed in 860-62/1456-58 and edited by Juynboll and Matthes in 2 volumes, Leyden 1855-61. It is a history of Egypt from 'Arab conquest to 1454. It records that news by fire signal used to reach Alexandria from Ceuta in one night. The Arabs had maintained this Greek system of fire signalling mainly throughout the North African coast.

Al-Juwaini's *Mawrid al-Latafa fi man waliya'l-saltana wa'l Khilafa* is a short history of Prophet Muḥammad, his compainions and of Egyptian rulers and their wazirs. Maqrīzī's *al-Sulūk* was continued by him for the years 845-860 (1441-1456) under the title of *Hawadith al-duhūr fi ma' laiyain wa'l shuhūr.*

Jalāluddin al-Suyūtī (1445-1505 A.D.) became known as such after the name of his birth place Suyūt (Usuit) in Upper Egypt. From his father side he was a Persian although his mother was an admixture of Turkish blood. His father died while he was only of about six years old and despite his precarious condition the orphan boy got by heart the whole of the *Qura'n* before he reached the age of eight years. He completed his education under the guidance of renowned teachers and served as Professor at Cairo until 1501. He retired to the island of Rawdah on the Nile and died four years later. He wrote many pamphlets and books numbering 500 on the *Qura'n*, *ḥadith*, *fiqh* (theology), philosophy, history, philology and rhetoric many of which were the outcomes of his polygraphic practices usual with many authors of the time. Although his writings were not generally of original character he was prolific writer like Ibn al-Jawzi, Ibn Hazm and al-Tabari. For his writings he became known throughout the Islamic world from India to Morocco popularising the scientific culture of his time in the 15th century. Among his known works are the *Tafsiru'l Jalalayn*, *al-Itqan fi 'Ulūm al-Qura'n*, a commentary of the *Qura'n*, the *Muzhir* (*Mizhar*) a treatise on philology, the *Husnu'l Muhadarah fi Akhbar Misr al-Qahirah*, a history of Egypt and that of old and new Cairo and the *Tari'khu'l Khulafa'* (History of the Caliphs). In his *Husnu'l Muhadarah*, Suyūtī mentions about the provisions made for the incapacitated and limbless persons and the appointment of servants to assist the blind and the incapacitated persons. The author informs about Ma'mūn's qādī in Egypt drawing a monthly salary of 4,000 dirhams.

CHAPTER II

ADMINISTRATION UNDER THE PROPHET AND THE PIOUS CALIPHS

'Arab Tribes:—The Ancient Arabs were divided into two categories the *Ahl al-Hadarah* (the Town people) and *Ahl al-Badiyah* (the Desert dwellers). The natural facilities available to the two groups and their economic activities being different, there was a remarkable difference in their governmental organisations which had direct bearing on the growth and development of 'Arab administration.

The Ancient 'Arab States:—From very ancient times the *Ahl al-Hadarah* (the Town people) of South Arabia had their kingdoms of Ma'ia between Najran and Himyar with Qararua as its capital and al-Yaman with Sirwah as its capital followed by the rule of the Himyarit dynasty in Saba' and Dhu-Raydan with an interval of the Abyssinians rule in Yaman between 340-378 A.D and final occupation of Yaman by the Abyssinian general Abraha in 525. In 575 Sayf him Dhi Yazm with the Persian aid received from Kisra Anushirwan drove the Abyssinians out of the country and since then the South Arabia went under the influence of the Persians.

Meanwhile because of the break up of the great dam Ma'rib from time to time and its final collapse in between 542 and 570 Yaman suffered from inundations and some tribes moved to the North. The South Arabs who migrated to the North established two important kingdoms. In the west of the Euphrates the kingdom of al-Hirah was founded by Banu Tanukh in the beginning of the second century of Christian era and ruled by the Lakhmid dynasty as a vassal of the Persian Empire. Towards the north-west of the Hirah the Ghassanids ruled as vassals of the Byzantine Emperors having capitals at al-Jabiyah and Jilliq. They were more powerful and civilized than the Lakhmids were. While the Lakhmids became known for learning and writing the

Ghassanids built palaces with columns of hewn stones and towers of victories and patronised poets.

The City State of Makkah:—Makkah because of being trade centre enjoyed material prosperity and further because of the Ka'bah it enjoyed social prestige and was quite distinct from other cities of Arabia. The city administration was run by a Council of Elders called al-Mala'.[1] To transact business the leading citizen met in a hall called Daru'n Nadwah and the general meeting of the citizens (*nadiu qawm*) took place in the court of the Ka'bah.[2] Functions relating to the city in general and the Ka'bah in particular were entrusted to leading Makkan families as the Quraysh being incharge of the Ka'bah.

For the safe passage of their caravans the Makkans concluded treaties with the neighbouring states, the Shaykhs of the Najd, the Lakhmid and the Ghassanid princes, the Persian and Byzantine Emperors and the Negus of Abyssinia. The trade caravans passing through Makkah paid tithe on their merchandise. Daru'n Nadwah was the head quarters of the Makkan trade caravans whose number swelled sometimes to 300 men and 2,500 camels [3] They carried on partnership business and the whole population of Makkah participated in internal and external trade in one way or the other by supplying water and food or leading the caravans through dangerous routes with the cooperation of the local chiefs.

The Shaykhs :—Among the desertmen (*Ahl al-Badiyah*) there was no elaborate machinery of administration, no officials or offices but there was a ruler in each clan and tribe. He was called al-Shaykh (the Elder) The 'Arab Chief represented the united will of the tr be both in peace and war. He was elected in times of war and he generally imposed his will on his followers (tribesmen) during peace time but he had no power to lay duties or inflict punishment on them. The Shaykh did not possess any executive power and as such the tribe did not have any criminal law.

Nobility of birth, seniority in age and personal distinctions determine d his position in the po itical society of the tribe. His

1. Al-Baladhuri, p. 52.
2. Cf. 'Macc a' in *Encyclopaedia of Islam.*
3. *Ibid.*

tenure of office depended on the good will of his constituency. The Arabs being democratic in spirit were averse to submit to the arbitrary rules of the Shaykh. Hence he had to make his decision in *al-Mala'* (a council of the Elders in the town) which represented the clans and sub-clans. Every clan was responsible for the conduct of its members. Maintenance of peace within the tribe was the prime responsibility of the Shaykh which he did, assisted by the council of Elders. In judicial, military and other affairs of common concern he had to consult with the tribal council represented by the heads of the component families. As the 'Arabs were born democrats the family heads met their Shaykh on an equal footing. Although the council was not strictly a representative body yet it acted as a check upon the arbitrary power of the Shaykh. If the Shaykh, however, happened to be powerful he overruled the decision of the Elders. He settled disputes within the tribe even differences between husband and wife and protected the tribe from external aggression. Punishment of murder, theft and adultery was severe. If the culprit escaped, he found no protection and no safety and was declared *al-tarīd* (an outlaw).

The Shaykh was the civil and military leader. The tribe being mostly engaged in constant tribal wars, each 'Arab was trained to be a soldier. Only the rich could afford to own horses as they were scarce in Arabia before Islām. Booty was equally divided among all the soldiers. The Shaykh received one-fourth of the whole booty *(al-mirha')*, the articles he liked most *(al-safaya')*,, rare articles like horses which could not be distributed equally (*al-fudūl*) and the valuables obtained while on the march (*al-Nashitah*) while the soldier who killed an enemy received all his accoutrement (*al-salab*) in addition to his share in the booty. Among the offensive weapons the Arabs used were swords, lances, bows and arrows while the defensive ones were shields and coats of mail, the latter being used only by the rich . orses, being scarce in the country, were used only for sudden attack and flight (*al-karr* and *al-farr*).

The individual was free with the exception of traditional practices concerning marriage or rights of property. He was free to withdraw from one tribe and join another by attaching himself to a member of that tribe. He was responsible for the duties for which he voluntered himself. Tribal society consisted of the chief and his family, *halif* (one who has taken an oath) and *mulsaq* (one who is attached), *mawla* (the freedmen) and the slaves, governed by uncodified ordinances. The *mawla* of a family was the *mawla* of the clan and the tribe to which the family belonged and was a great asset to the family.

Virtues and Vices;—The clan organization was the basis of the 'Arab Bedouin society. Every tent represented a family and every encampment of tents or groups of tents was called *al-hayy* (clan). A number of clans (*qawm*) or a number of kindred grouped together fromed a *qabilah* (tribe). The pastures and cultivated fields were held in common by the tribe. Among the cardinal virtues of the old Bedouin Arabs were unswerving loyalty to kinsmen and ruthlessness in avenging any wrong or insult done to one's self or one's relations or tribesmen. The Arabs had such a strong family and tribal attachment called *'Aṣabiyah* that they sacrificed their own personal interests for the greater cause of the clan and the tribe. The Bedouin was obliged to stand by his brother and clan member in distress without questioning whether he was in the right or wrong. "Be loyal to the tribe", says an 'Arab poet, "its claim upon its members is strong enough to make a husband give up his wife."[1] Some small tribes had fromed confederacies (*al-ahlaf*) for their protection and safety.

On the growth in number of the family members the tribe used to go out of the control of the chief Shaykhs, dissensions would set in an secession took place.[2] In spite of speaking the same language and following the same manners and customs their groupings and love of independence were great obstacles in the way of their unity. On some insignificant matter they were prepared to separate and fight for years together. The Arabs were known for love of independence and bravery, implacable desire for vengeance and protection of the week, qualities of survival in the desert which were exploited fully to the advantage of Islam by

1. Al-Mubarrad, *al-Kamil*, ed. W. Wright, Leipzig, 1864, p. 229 quoted by Hitti, *History of the Arabs*, p. 27n. 3.
2. Cf. Author's *A Political History of the Muslims*, vol. I, pp. XVII-XVIII.

Prophet Muḥammad and his successors with modifications and infusion of new spirit of Islam into them. The tribal feeling based on blood relationship which binds families into clans and clans into tribes gradually gave way to the more individualistic social organisation in Islam.

Women had no distinct position in ancient 'Arab society. Their lives and honour were of little consequence. Even married women were given freely to guests and strangers. As pastime the nobles often tied women to the tails of a galloping horse crushing them to death. They, however, received dowry and acquired wealth although they did not have the right of inheritance. Gambling and drunkness were common. On default in the payment of loans the creditor took possession of the wives and children of the borrowers and sold them into slavery. These were the vices in the 'Arab society and there was need of reform and modification in the nomadic ethics.

The Prophet :- Prophet Muḥammad came and taught that Islām must take precedence over tribal loyalties and created a society governed by codified ordinances. Now differences began to be recorded between believers and non-believers and not between one tribe and another and their hitherto nomadic and uncheque-red life began to change into settled life and the whole population came to be organised into a religio-militia.

The civil laws affecting the individual, and particularly the inheritance, were introduced. In 3H/624-5 one of the main provisions of inheritance emerged when Sa'd's widow complained to the Prophet against the seizure of the property of her husband by his brother and according to the decree of the Prophet, she received one-eighth of the property, her two daughters one-third each and Sa'ds brother the remainder. Islam "aimed at eliminating the abuses which arose in the change from a communal system of ownership to an individualistic one." The reforms introduced for the security of life and property were fully effective and substituted the uneasy bills passed during the raids with social security. While usury was forbidden, profit-making from trade was encouraged. The payment of *zakat* by rich to the poor helped in maintaining economic and social equilibrium. A code was drawn up by the Prophet concerning contributions in kind, in cash a camel being equal to ten sheep and a sheep to twenty dirhams.

On migration to Madinah Prophet Muḥammad's great task was to modify the nomadic ethics in order to suit the new environment and society. The Prophet established firm brotherhood between the Anṣars (the helpers) and the Muhajirs (the refugees), who were then only forty-five in number and each refugee was associated with a helper so much so that the helper apportioned his refugee associate an equal share in all his belongings.[1] The Anṣars being agriculturists, in the main, cultivated mostly date palm and barley and gave their Muhajir brethren equal shares in the produce. In the same way as the Anṣars were prepared to make sacrifices for their refugee-co-religonists, the Muhajirs were reluctant to exploit this fact to their own advantage. The refugees being essentially artisans and traders started cottage industries, engaged themselves in trade and began to earn their own living. Abu Bakr had his industry at Sakh[2] and 'Abd al-Rahman ibn 'Awf set up his own independent business in the market of Qaynuqā'.[3] 'Umar and 'Uthman also carried on trade.[4] Soon the Muhajirs attained self sufficiency and affluence and contributed their bit to the *Bayt al-Mal* (Public Treasury) instituted for communal welfare in 9 A.H.

The Charter of Madinah :—The Prophet next turned his attention to the establishment of friendly relations among the various tribes of Madinah, *viz*,. the heathen tribes of Banu Aws and Banu Khazraj who formed the majority of the population and accepted Islam in large number and the Jewish tribes Banu Qurayzah, Banu Nadir and Banu Qaynuqa'.[5] The Jews never liked the unity and amity of the Anṣars and the Muhajirs and the Muslims were still a minority at Madinah. To maintain internal peace and keep Madinah secure from external aggression, particulary of the Makkans, Prophet Muḥammad approached the Jews with open arms, recognizing their religion and calling the Jews and the

1. Cf. Ibn Hisham, p. 179; Shibli, I, 288-292.
2. Cf. Ibn Sa'd, III, p. 130 quoted by Shibli, p. 287.
3. Cf. *Usudal Ghabah*, IV, pp. 314-5.
4. *Musnad Ibn Hanbal*, VI, pp. 347, 400.
5. Cf. Ibn Ishaq, p. 372/253 tr.

Muslims together within six months of the Hijri era, dictated a constitution which came to be known as the Charter of Madinah. Ibn Isḥaq says, "This is a document from Muḥammad the Prophet (governing the relations) between the believers and Muslims of Quraysh and Yathrib and those who followed them and joined them and laboured with them."[1]

Thus the various Jewish clans were blended together with the Muslims under the leadership of Prophet Muḥammad into a community (*Ummah*). The feuding code was also listed and the murderer was subjected to blood vengeance and deprived of any quarter. The Jews and the Muslims were to resist external attacks as one community. In case of war, if the city was attacked, the Jews were obliged to contribute towards war funds though not compelled to participate actively in the war. The guarantee of peace and protection of life, property, sanctity of women and liberty were all incorporated in the Charter of Madinah. Thus Madinah was assured of peace and prosperity as long as the citizens remained loyal to the terms of the charter. The referring of disputes to Prophet Muḥammad by the Muslims and the Jews according to the term no. 42 was to the recognition of Prophet's right to administer justice among the confeuding Madinites according to the Divine Law.[2] The Jews, however, gradually understood the teachings and practices of Islam and their significance and when Prophet's teachings did not meet their traditional religious concepts they became alarmed for the preservation of their own faith and power and while they began to dishonour their commitments their *rabbis* harassed the Prophet with their disputations and abusive verses leading to the expulsion of the Jews from Madinah.

Prophet Muḥammad gave Arabia a centralized form of government which concentrated a good deal of power in its hands retaining many of its ancient laws, institutions and customs. From the Charter of Madīnah it is clear that the Prophet did not like to brush aside the old tribal constitution but he wanted to adopt, expand and reform it since the tribal organisation was inadequate for the large growing community of Islām. It contains

1. Ibn Ishaq, pp. 341-4/231-33, tr. ; Ibn Hisham, I, pp. 278-9; Shibli, I, 296; Watt, *Muhammad at Madinah*, pp. 221-25.
2. Ibn Ishaq, p. 343/233; Watt, p. 224.

the germ of the Islamic State founded by the Prophet with adequate provisions for legislative functions but left in a rudimentary condition as far as judicial and executive functions were concerned. Tribal chiefs lost their pre-eminence and were brought under the banner of one, Prophet Muḥammad, who received guidance from Allah to govern the community and the individual members composing the Islamic community had to relinquish a good portion of their freedom and bow to Him and obey His vice-gerent who was the Head of the state and the spiritual leader of the community. Sovereignty lies with Allah in Islam and Prophet Muḥammad was His vice-gerent.

The authority of the Prophet was supreme in executing the injuctions of the *Qur'an* and in matters on which there was no light from the Holy Book. Although in fact he was fully sovereign he usually consulted his chief companions on all important matters. He held his office in the Masjid al-Nabawī.

The Prophet's secretariate began to function in its elementary form during his lifetime. The Divine revelations were recorded by 'Alī and 'Uthmān and. in their absence, by Zayd b. Thābit and Ubayy b. Ka'ab.[1] The entry of *amwal al-ṣadaqat* (properties collected by way of *zakat* and *ṣadaqah*) was made by al-Zubayr b. al-'Awwām and al-Juhaym b. al-Salt.[2] The registrars of transactions made between the people were al-Mughīrah b. Shu'ayb and al-Hasan b. Namir and revenue official was Hudhayfah b. al-Yamān who prepared estimates of revenue from the date-palms earned by people. The record of *Ghanimah* was maintained by Mu'ayqib b. Abi Fāṭimah. 'Alā b. 'Uqbah and Allah b. 'Abd al-Arqam maintained records of the Anṣārs and of the tribes and their waters.[3] Letters addressed to Kings and Chiefs were drafted by Zayd b. Thābit[4] and sometimes by 'Abd Allāh ibn al-Arqam while the Prophet's seal was kept by Hanzalah b. al-Rabi.[5]

The Caliph :—Prophet Muḥammad's Khalīfahs (successors) inherited his full powers on the secular side and a vestige of his

1. Al-Jahshiyari, p. 11
2. *Ibid.*, p. 11
3. *Ibid.*, pp. 11-12
4. *Ibid.*, p. 12
5. *Ibid.*, p. 12.

religious authority. The *Amirs* (Governors) appointed by the Prophet and his successors were the real rulers of the provinces.

On the demise of Prophet Muḥammad when some Anṣar Chiefs of the Banu Khazraj tribe were heard to have met to elect a chief some Muhajir chiefs including Hadrat Abū Bakr, 'Umar and Abu 'Ubaydah hurriedly joined the meeting and after some discussions Abu Bakr being the most suitable in the community was elected khalīfah (substitute of Prophet Muḥammad). As during Prophet Muḥammad's last illness Abu Bakr had been ordered by the Prophet himself to lead the five times prayer in the Masjid al-Nabawi in his stead it facilitated his election. In the following morning Abu Bakr sat on the *minbar* (pulpit) of the Masjid al-Nabawi and 'Umar called upon the people to swear allegiance to Abu Bakr. Those who had been present in the meeting the previous night renewed their oath of allegiance and others present then followed the suit clasping Abu Bakr by hand. Hadrat Abu Bakr nominated 'Umar as his successor as his active participation in the administration during the caliphate of Abu Bakr and his prominent position had clearly marked him out as the ultimate successor. The Arabs were familiar with both these types of election and nomination from pre-Islamic period. On receiving mortal wound at the hand of an assassin and finding none of extraordinary calibre Hadrat 'Umar nominated a council of six members from the council of Elders to elect one among themselves as caliph assuming that such an election would have the confidence and support of at least five other influential companions of the Prophet and their men. Prince Caetani a great authority on Islam expresses doubt and says that it was a later invention made during the Abbasids to justify their nomination of a successor and opines that like the Prophet Hadrat 'Umar died leaving the matter of election entirely in the hands of those concerned.[1] Arnold observes that there was certainly some form of election in the case of Abu Bakr, 'Umar, 'Uthman and 'Ali and that there was no consideration of relationship in the choice of a caliph.[2]

Prophet Muḥammad besides performing prophetic functions

1 *Annali del' Islam*, 11 A.H. 55 sqq and 13 A.H. 75 sqq. 133 sqq. quoted by Sir Thomos W. Arnold., *The Caliphate*, 1967, p. 21.

2. Arnold, p. 22.

had been the head of state as well as of the church. As successor of the Prophet, Hadrat Abu Bakr performed all his functions except the prophetic ones and preferred to be described by the modest title of *Khalifat Rasul Allah* (successor of the Apostle of God) and not as *Khalifah* of Allah.[1] Succeeding Abu Bakr in 634 'Umar styled himself *Khalifah of the Khalifah of the Apostle of God* but finding it lengthy he decided to be called *khalifah* only and assumed the title of *Amiru'l Mu'minin* (the commander of the faithfuls) with certain hesitation. 'Umar's successors also called themselves *Amiru'l Mu'minin.* The pious caliphs were described by either one of the three titles *khalifah, Amiru'l Mu'minin* or *Imam.* While *khalifah* lays emphasis on his relation with the Prophet, the title *Amiru'l Mu'minin* asserts his relation with the faithfuls over whom he rules and whom he defends and the title *Imam* lays stress on his relation with the religion of Islam as religious head. *Imam* is more significant to the Shi'ahs than to the Sunnis as the former ascribe supernatural power to him and consider him even incarnation of God.

There was neither hierarchy nor priesthood in Islām. Personal merit, seniority, position, relationship to the Prophet, tribal backing and past services to Islām were the factors taken into consideration in the election or nomination of a Khalīfah. The Khalīfah thus elected was the temporal head without any independent religious authority.

Abū Bakr and 'Umar were of the Quraysh descent and the third Khalīfah elected was 'Uthmān ibn 'Affān, an Umayyad, also belonged to the Quraysh. Due to misunderstanding, trouble arose towards the end of his Khilāfat leading to his murder and the election of 'Alī and practically the office was thrust on him by the insurgents. 'Ali's supporters considered that he, being not only a son-in-law of the Prophet like Hadrat 'Uthmān but also a cousin to Muḥammad, had a prior claim to be Caliph. Thus the seeds of dissension having been once sown the community split up into two groups never to unite again. 'Uthmān's assassination created a party against 'Ali which rallied round the banner of his relative Amīr Mu'āwiyah of Syria who held 'Alī responsible for

1. Kanz, III, 2237.

the murder of Hadrat 'Uthmān. At the first opportunity, he proclaimed himself caliph of Syria bifurcating the Islamic world into two Caliphates during the last days of Hadrat 'Ali, one at Damascus and the other at Kūfah. 'Alī's main support had been at Madīnah but he had transferred his capital to Kūfah on the Euphrates to have more support from the Irāqīs the enemies of the Syrians and thus to overpower Mu'āwiyah. 'Abd Allāh ibn Sabā's propaganda against 'Uthmān and in favour of 'Alī, the *wasī* (executor) of Prophet Muḥammad, had its effects on the 'Irāqīs who were favourably disposed towards the hereditary principle of the Persians. Hadrat 'Alī was murdered by the Khārijites who regarded both 'Alī and Mu'āwiyah as usurpers but their attack on Mu'āwiyah did not prove fatal.

'Alī was succeeded by his son Hasan at Kūfah but he abdicated soon in favour of Mu'āwiyah who, in his turn, held that the stability of the government could not be maintained in a democratic system. In order to ensure stability he thought of continuing the *Khilafat* in his line and therefore nominated his son Yazīd as *walī 'ahd* (successor) against the wishes of the populace of Madīnah and Makkah. Thus in the provinces *ba'yt* was taken at the hands of the governors and other officials on behalf of Yazīd. Hasan, son of 'Alī, and 'Abd Allāh ibn Zubayr, the two rivals of Yazīd established themselves one after another at Kūfah and Makkah in opposition to the Umayyad Khilāfat at Damascus. Yazīd was accepted ruler of Syria and 'Abd Allāh of the Hijāz and Egypt. It was 'Abd al-Malik, the fourth ruler of the Umayyad dynasty, who killd Ibn Zubayr in a battle and established his authority over all the Muslim territories. Thus the hereditary system of succession in which son or brother, on the basis of seniority or ability, used to be nominated by the dying Caliph was established and this continued throughout the reign of the Umayyads.

The Khilāfat of Abū Bakr is significant for the establishmen of peace within Arabia, the repulse of the foreign aggressors and the introduction of social and political institutions but the foundation of the actual government and proper administration was laid during the time of Hadrat 'Umar. The latter believed in giving right to all to demand and safeguard his or her right and to express his views openly, to limit the righis of the ruler and to criticize his action. 'Umar himself summed up the rights and duties of the Caliph and the subjects. The Caliph had his share in the wealth of the subjects as the guardian had in that of the orphans. If he was affluent he should take nothing from it and if he was poor he should take according to his needs. The subjects had the right to know that the revenue and booty were spent in a befitting manner, to demand the increase of the daily rations, to guard the frontiers and to protect them from danger. These duties and responsibilities he acknowledged and discharged. Once, while 'Umar was discoursing on the rates of dowry, a woman intervened and commented that he had no right to fix that which had been kept open by God for negotiations between the two parties. 'Umar stopped and said, "Even a woman knows more than I do." It happened once that Hafṣah, his daughter and widow of the Prophet, came to demand a share in the booty recently received on the ground of her being a close relation. 'Umar commented that as his daughter she had claim in his personal property but not in that of the common fund of the Muslims.[1] On another occasion 'Umar fell ill and people prescribed honey for him. There was honey in the *Bayt al-Mal* but he would not take even a drop of it except with the permission of the assembly in the Mosque.

The Caliph's orders were binding only to the extent that they did not contravene the prescriptions of the *Qura'n* and the *Hadīth*. In matters which did not find direction either from the *Qura'n* or the *Hadīth* he had to abide by the decisions of the Council of Elders and theologians. Abū Bakr had limited his own authority in holding office as long as he proved himself worthy of the same. 'Umar declared, "There can be no Khilāfat except by consultation."[2] In the *Majlis al-Shūra* once called in to decide as to whether or not the conquered territories of 'Irāq and Syria were to be distributed among Muslim soldiers. 'Umar spoke, "Verily I do not implore you but to share with one in the

1. *Kitab al-Kharaj*, 67.
2. *Al-Faruq*, II, 17.

task entrusted to me and the burden of your affairs and that you should follow anything arising out of my caprice."[1]

'Umar initiated and encouraged democratic methods in the appointment of tax-collectors. It was on the willingness of the people of the localities concerned, 'Uthmān b. al-Farqad, al-Hajjāj b. al-Illāt and Ma'an b. Yazīd were appointed tax-collectors of Kūfah, Baṣrah and Damascus respectively. It was this weakness of 'Umar which emboldened the citizens of Kūfah and Baṣrah to demand the frequent changes of Governors and create dissensions during the Khilāfat of 'Uthmān.

Abū Bakr had appointed 'Umar chief justice and entrusted him with the distribution of *zakat* and 'Alī was placed in charge of the supervision of the captives of war and of correspondence thus sharing in the administration of the newly created Muslim State with his chief companions.

'Umar's Khilafāt was akin to a republican form of Government. All matters relating to the country and the nation were discussed in the *Majlis al-Shūra* and resolutions were adopted. It was constituted by the elders of the *Muhajirs* and the *Anṣars* for transacting ordinary business. To assist him in the administration of day-to-day affairs, 'Umar had an inner council of his Chief companions and advisers,[2] 'Uthmān, 'Alī, 'Abd al-Rahmān b. 'Awf, Ma'ādh b. Jabal, Ibn Abī K'ab and Zayd b. Thābit.

Besides this *Majlis al-Shūra*, Council of the Elders, there was another council constituted by the members hailing from all tribes, the Muhājirs and the Anṣārs, which was called in to decide certain serious, important and unusual issues such as the question of the distribution of the conquered land among the soldiers,[3] and the sessions continued for days together, and finally, it resolved against it. And again it was the Council of Elders which dissuaded 'Umar from taking the command of the Muslim force in person in the battle of Nahāwand.[4]

For holding the meeting of *Majlis al-Shūra*, a herald used to go round proclaiming *al-Salat Jami'ah*. People used to gather in

1. Abu Yusuf, p. 14.
2. Baladhuri, *Futuh al-Buldan*, 276.
3. *Ibid.*, 269; Abu Yusuf, pp. 12, 14, 15.
4. Tabari, I, 2214-18.

the Mosque and 'Umar after performing two rak'ats of *ṣalat* used to address the gathering on the necessity for having called the meeting and then he invited suggestions from every member present.[1] The fixation of the salary of soldiers, appointments of governors and officials and rights of foreign merchants trading in Muslim lands and such other matters used to be the items of agenda before the council.

The Walī:—Prophet Muḥammad began to administer his newly-created State from his headquarters at Madīnah. To enable the establishment of law and order in distant regions, the country was divided into the provinces of al-Madīnah, Makkah, Tayma', al-Janad, Najrān, al-Yaman, Hadramawt, 'Umān, al-Baḥrayn and the region of Banū Kindah and a *Walī* (Governor) was appointed to rule over each province.

After the conquest of Syria and Persia 'Umar redivided the empire into fourteen provinces in Madīnah, Makkah, Syria, Jazīrah (Mesopotamia proper), Baṣrah, Kūfah, Egypt, Palestine, Khurāsān, Ādharbayjān, Mikrān, Kirmān, Sijistān and Fārs. Palestine was divided into two sub-provinces with their governors at Ayliya and Ramlah. Similarly Egypt was divided into Upper and Lower provinces with separate Governors, Ibn Abī Sharh and 'Amr ibn al-'Āṣ, the latter being also Governor-General.

The high officials of the centre and provinces were selected in the *Majlis al-Shūra*. 'Umar with due considerations used to propose the names and they were seconded and approved by the members of the *Shūra*. Thus Nu'mān b. Miqrān was selected for the expedition on Nahāwand. Among the provincial officials were Hākim (governor), *Katib* (secretary), *Katib al-Dīwan* (military secretary), *Saḥib al-Kharaj* (revenue collectors), *Saḥib al-Aḥdath* (police officer), *Sahib Bayt al-Mal* (treasurer) and Qādī (judge). Tabarī[2] preserves the names of the provincial officers of Kūfah *viz*., governor 'Ammār b. Yasir, revenue collector 'Uthmān b. Hanīf, treasurer 'Abd Allāh ibn Mas'ūd, military secretary 'Abd Allāh b. Khuzā'i and judge Sharīḥ.

The *Walī* was the representative of the Caliph in the province

1. Tabari, 2574.
2. *Ibid*., 2641.

and hence he ruled over the province on his behalf leading the prayers in the mosque and commanding soldiers in the battle-field. He was responsible for maintaining peace within his jurisdiction and for protecting the frontiers from foreign aggression. On the appointment of *Walī* people gathered in the Masjid al-Nabawi and 'Umar used to address the Governors in front of the audience thus, "Listen, verily I am not sending you as the leaders of guidance so that men may follow you. Render unto the Muslims their rights; beat them not, lest you humiliate them; praise them not, lest you make them indisciplined. Do not shut your doors against them lest the strong amongst them devour the weak ones."[1] On arrival at his headquarters, the Governor used to read the contents of the letter of appointment before the populace at his headquarters so that his powers and duties and their own rights and obligations would be made known to them.

Peace and Justice: – In the pre-prophetic period of Muḥammad there was a confederacy of the Quraysh in Makkah known as *Hilf al-Fudūl*. It had been set up to repress the oppressors and protect the rights of every weak man in the city. On his migration to Madīnah the Prophet granted a charter to the Jews strengthening the hand of the law-abiding citizens and obliging them to hand over the offender alone to the victim or his avenger. This was a clear departure from the old 'Arab practice of inflicting retaliation even on the relatives of the wrongdoer. Thus blood-feuds within the community were completely stopped and the offender was brought before the Caliph for his decision before the payment of the penalty. The Prophet and his Khalifahs were responsible for the maintenance of internal discipline. On the expansion of Empire they delegated their power to the governors and judicial officers of the provinces.

Prophet Muḥammad was himself the chief justice and, to assist him in administering justice, he appointed judges in the provinces or directed the governors to appoint persons named by him. The judges were independent of the governors in the matter of dispensing justice. This shows that even during his time the judiciary was separated from the executive. Eminent scholars of

1. Abu Yusuf, p. 66.

exemplary character were appointed as *Qadis* and they treated the
high and the low as equals before the law.[1] The judges were paid
handsomely in order to dissuade them from thinking of accepting
bribes. The judges like Salmān, Rabi'ah and S̲h̲ariḥ received 500
dirhams each monthly[2] while Mu'āwiyah received 1,000 dīnārs a
month. No case of the Qadi's accepting bribe, in the days of the
pious Caliphs, was ever reported. The mosque was used as the
court of justice and in order not to deter even the poorest person
seeking justice, the courts were free for all and no court fee
whatever was charged.

To pronounce on disputed matters and problems and pass
decrees on such, the Department of *Ifta'* was established. During
the time of 'Umar the members of this body were 'Ut̲h̲mān, 'Ali,
Abū Hurayrah, Ma'ād̲h̲ b. Jabal, 'Abd al-Raḥmān b. 'Awf, Ibn
Abi K'ab, Zayd ibn T̲h̲ābit and Abū Dardā.

Police :—To establish peace and order a police (*Aḥdat̲h̲*)
department was established with *Sahib al-Ahdat̲h̲* (*S̲h̲urtah*) as its
chief officer. In the beginning of Muslim rule generally the duties of
the Police were performed by the people. The Prophet appointed
Abū Hurayrah with police duties in al-Baḥrayn. 'Umar introduced
night watches and patrols and 'Ali introduced for the first time the
office of the *S̲h̲urtah* (a police-cum-municipal department) on a
regular basis. The primary duty of the police was to maintain
and restore peace within the city. It had its branches in all
provincial and important towns. In small cities there were soldiers
called the *ma'ūnah* to maintain peace. They made nocturnal
rounds for detecting thiefs and malefactors. The chief officer of
this force was the *Sahib al-S̲h̲urtah* (prefect of police) or *Sahib al-
Ma'ūnah* charged with the police duties in the city. In times of
war or unrest he had to organize the main body of the troops.
The *ahdat̲h̲* or foot soldiers were posted in the outlying districts to
maintain law and order and to fight battle when needed.

The police was also entrusted with the work of ḥisbah
(municipal and market affairs). They were to see that proper
weights and measures were used in the markets, houses were not

---

1. Jurji Zaydan, *Ta'rikh al-Tammadun al-Islami*, IV, 39.
2. *Hidayah*, II, 247.

constructed on roads and public places, animals were not laden with heavy loads and wine was not sold publicly. In short they were to look after the interest of the public and to help in the preservation of public morals.

The *Sahib al-Shurtah* (the Chief Police officer) investigated offences committed, made his decisions in accordance with the political and customary law and punished the guilty. The religious side of the law was interpreted by the Qādi who determined the appropriate punishment and prescribed legal penalties. Unlike the *Qadī* the *Sahib al-Shurtah* enjoyed power to extract confession from an accused person by force.

Imprisonment and expulsion were introduced by 'Umar as punishments for misconduct. The first prison was made at Makkah after purchasing the house of Safwān b. Ummiyah for 4,000 dirhams.[1] Other prisons were constructed in the districts. Abū Mahjan Thaqafī was banished to an island for the offence of being a habitual drunkard.[2]

'*Āmil*: —To collect taxes specially *zakat* (poor-rate) and *ṣadaqah* (voluntary alms), 'Amils known for their integrity were appointed in the provinces by the Prophet. Under the pious Caliphs each province had *Dar al-Amarat* (a permanent Government House) and *al-Dīwan* (a permanent Secretariat) and the provinces were divided into districts which again were divided into sub-divisions to each of which an '*Āmil* was posted. On the appointment of an '*Āmil* or *Walī* his powers and duties were specified and he had to furnish a detailed list of his properties and belongings.[3] Before appointment the tax-collector had to undertake to be honest in his dealings and not to use Turkish horses, or fine dress; nor was he to eat bread made of fine flour and keep a gate-keeper.[4]

When 'Umar was received in Syria by Muslim officials clad in silken robes he became angry and reprimanded them. 'Ayyād b. Ghanam the '*Āmil* of Egypt wore fine dress and kept a guard at his gate. It was repo ed to 'Umar who ordered Muhammad b. Muslimah to enquire into the matter and present the '*Āmil* before

1. Maqrizi, II, 187
2. *Usud al-Ghabah* see Abu Mahjan Thaqafi
3. Baladhuri, 219
4. Tabari, 2747.

him. He was ordered to put off his fine dress and proceed to graze sheep. On imploring forgiveness he was pardoned and as long as he lived he performed his duties efficiently.[1]

On an extraordinary increase in the property of the '*Āmil* the excessive wealth as that of Abū Hurayrah and 'Amr b. al-'Āṣ was confiscated by 'Umar.[2] Once a large number of '*Āmils* were found profiteering in business. Khālid b. Sa'd composed a poem on this and reported the matter to 'Umar. The wealth of all was assessed and half of their properties were confiscated by the State.

There was a general circular for people to place their grievances against the tax-collectors before the Khalīfah during the time of *ḥajj* where 'A*mils* were instructed to be present on the occasion and the sufferers were compensated. Once a person reported that one of the '*Āmils* had beaten him. Mustaghīth was ordered to punish him with 100 lashes. 'Amr b. al-'Āṣ pleaded for him but Hadrat 'Umar did not listen. Then 'Amr b. al-'Āṣ made Mustaghīth accept two dinars for each stripe.[3] The famous general Khālid b. Walīd was deposed because he gave a handsome present to a poet and was found guilty of extravagance, if not of embezzlement.[4] To dissuade the officers from accepting bribe, they were paid handsomely and provided with rations. 'Ammār b. Yasir had an annuity of 600 dirhams and received as daily rations, wheat,and mutton.[5]

There was no state treasury during the time of the Prophet. Whatever came as booty or revenue were distributed then and there by him. In the second year of the Khilāfat, Abū Bakr built a treasury but there was only one dirham in it at the time of his death. Following Prophet Muḥammad, he distributed all what he received, ten dirhams to every one in the first year and twenty in the second year of his Khilāfat.

Hadarat 'Umar took census of the Muslims and established a *Dīwan* a Persian institution[6] to register the names of the receipients of pensions. Hadrat 'Ā'ishah topped the list and received 12,000

1. Tabari, 2403.
2. *Kitab al-Kharaj*, 66
3. Baladhuri, 82-3, 291
4. *Kitab al-Kharaj*, 66
5. Ibn Athir, II, 418
6. *Orient Under the Caliphs*, 112.

dirhams annually. According to the gradations, the *ahl-bayt*, emigrants and helpers received 4,000 to 5,000 dirhams annuity. An ordinary soldier received 500 to 600 dirhams while women, children and clients received 200 to 300 dirhams a year. The treasury was reorganized and sub-treasuries were set up in provincial and district headquarters. 'Umar's proposal of founding a permanent treasury at Madīnah and its branches in the provinces was approved in the *Majlis al-Shūra* in about 15H/636 A.D. and the Hijrah era was introduced in the following year. The treasury officers were appointed and guards were posted by 'Umar. 'Abd Allāh b. al-Arqam was in-charge of *Bayt al Mal* and 'Abd al-Raḥmān b. 'Ubayd al-Qari and Mu'ayqib were appointed as his assistants. The treasury officers were generally independent of the governor and held an important position among the officials. Khālid b. Harith and 'Abd Allāh b. Mas'ūd were appointed treasurers in Iṣfahān and Kūfah respectively. They, after covering the expenditure of the provincial government, despatched the balance to the central *Bayt al-Mal* located at Madīnah which spent 3,00,000 dirhams on the salaries and pensions of the Madinites alone. Some slight changes were introduced in the Byzantine dīnār and Persian dirham retained in circulation by 'Umar and registers were maintained in Persian in 'Irāq and Persia, Syriac in Syria and Coptic in Egypt for recording revenues and expenditure.

Under Prophet Muḥammad there were five sources of revenue *viz.*, *al-Ghanīmah* (spoils of war), *al-Zakat* (poor-rate) and *al-Sadaqah* (voluntary alms). *al-Jizyah* (poll-tax), *al-Kharaj* (land-tax) and *al-Fayy'* (income from crown lands). On the expansion of the Empire under the pious Caliphs the revenue increased and a considerable additional income came from *al-'Ushūr* (the tithes) imposed on the merchandise for the first time by Hadrat 'Umar b. al-Khattab.

Al-Ghanimah (booty) comprised moveable property taken in battle from the non-Muslims. Inside Arabia, however, even landed property was included in the booty. The Prophet did not pay any salary to the soldiers but as the taxes came from ghanimah kharaj and jizyah they were distributed among the soldiers, bachelors receiving half of the share of married soldiers.

Four-fifths of the booty were distributed among the soldiers participating in the battle, a horseman receiving double the share of the foot-soldier,[1] and the soldier who killed an enemy received his accoutrements (*salab*), a pre-Islamic practice, in addition to his usual share in the booty. The remaining one-fifth (*Khums*) went to the State treasury and was divided into three shares, one being used in supporting the Prophet, another in supporting his relatives and the third spent on the orphans, the needy, wayfarers and for the general good of the Muslim community. Abū Bakr, 'Umar and 'Uthmān also divided the *khums* into three portions but spent the shares of the Prophet and his relatives on the equipment of army.[2] The prisoners taken in war were also distributed as slaves like other commodities of booty among the soldiers.[3] 'Umar enunciated that only moveable property and prisoners excluding money and land acquired in war were to be distributed among the warriors.

As ṣadaqah is a voluntary alms giving practice among the Muslims the *zakat* was levied on the properties of Muslims. It was a religio-state duty and paid on land produce immediately after the harvest and on cash, gold and silver after one year's uninterrupted possession. This tax was levied at the rate of 10 to 15% on the yield from land if this exceeded five *wasqs* (ass-loads, equal to 60 *sa'* or 323 lbs).[1] The minimum of gold and silver (*al-Nisab*) was the value of 200 dirhams and the rate was 2½%. The minimum numbers of camels and cattle on which *zakat* was levied being five and thirty respectively, the *zakat* for the former was a six-months old lamb or one-year old goat and for the latter, six months old calf. The rate of *zakat* was one year old cow for 40 to 59 cows and six-months lamb or one year old goat for 40 to 120 sheep. Horses were exempt from the *zakat* as they were scarce in Arabia during the time of the Prophet but with the increase in their trade after the conquest of 'Irāq and Persia the *zakat* was levied on them too by 'Umar. The income from the *zakat* was spent on the needy, indigent, collectors of *zakat*, the

1. Abu Yusuf, *Kitab al-Kharaj*, 11
2. *Ibid.*, 11-12
3. Cf. Mawardi, ch. XII.

emancipation of slaves, military enterprise, debtors, thieves and women of suspected character etc.

Like the Persian *gezit* and Román *tributum capiti* the Prophet realised *jizyah* at the rate of one *dīnar* per head per annum from Dhimmi (Protected non-Muslim) male members capable of paying it. Monks, beggars, women, children, the aged, the insane and the sick were, however, exempt. On the conquest of Syria, 'Irāq and Persia when conditions improved, 'Umar changed this uniform rate of *jizyah* and levied four *dinars*, two *dīnars* and one *dīnar* per annum according to payer's financial condition.[1] 'Amr b. al-'Āṣ, however, collected *jizyah* in Egypt at the uniform rate of two *dīnars* per head.

The *jizyah* being a military tax was collected only when the Muslims were sure of giving protection to life and property of the non-Muslims. Failing to protect the lives and properties of the people of Himṣ, Damascus, and other advance posts when the Muslims withdrew before the battle of Yarmūk, the *jizyah* already collected was returned.[2] No *jizyah* was collected from the Cypriots even after the conquest of Cyprus as Caliph 'Uthmān was not yet sure of giving them protection against the enemy's attack. *Dhimmis* taking part in a campaign were not required to pay *jizyah*. Once a *Dhimmi* on rendering some service to the Muslim army got exemption from the payment of *jizyah* for that year.[3]

The income from the *jizyah* and *kharaj* was spent on the maintenance of soldiers and other military purposes. The *kharaj* was the land-tax collected from non-Muslims. It was collected for the first time from the Jews of Khaybar at the rate of half of the produce and 'Abd Allah b. Rawāha was appointed to estimate the produce and collect the *kharaj*.[4] The land tax was collected by the Persians under the name of *kharaj* and by

1. Abu Yusuf, pp. 21, 31; Baladhuri, p. 7.
2. Baladhuri, 124, 152, 271, *jizyah* and *kharaj* were interchangeable terms in the beginning. In the general sense of tribute *jizyah* has been used in the Arabic papyri of the first century of Hijri and later *jizyah* has been called *kharaj 'ala ru'us ahl al-dhimmah* (a tax on the head of the protected people). In the narrower sense *jizyah* and *kharaj* have been used for the first time, it is said, by Abu Hanifah cf. Levy, *Social Structure of Islam*, p. 311 n. 1.
3. Baladhuri, 137; Abu Yusuf, 81.
4. Tabari, 2663-66.

the Romans under the head *tributum soli*. On the conquest of Khaybar the Jews recognised the ownership of the Muslim conquerors and offered to cultivate the lands as tenants and pay a portion of the produce as land-tax called *al-kharaj*. The Prophet accepted the offer as he did not have men to engage in cultivation. The old system of taxation in the non-'Arab conquered lands was retained and the *Marzubans* and *Dihqans* were allowed to retain their old rights. In some parts of the Sawād, the lower Euphrates-Tigris Valley, the Sassanids collected *kharaj* at the rate of one *qafīz* of grain and one dirham in cash per *jarīb* of land.[1] 'Umar appointed 'Uthmān b. Hunayf to survey the whole of 'Irāq. He surveyed 3,000 square miles with 36,000,000 *jaribs*[2] of cultivable lands. The rate of land-tax was revised and fixed according to the quality of land and the value of its produce. Thus the tax imposed was two dirhams per *jarīb* on barley, four on wheat, five on clove, six on sugar-cane, eight on date-palms and ten on grapes or fields with fruit trees.[3] This was not the uniform rate applicable to other places. The total revenue from 'Irāq in the year of survey was 86,000,000 dirhams which swelled and, according to Ibn Khurdādbih, amounted to 128,000,000 dirhams during the time of Hadrat 'Umar.[4] This was the result of bringing into cultivation waste lands mainly by digging irrigation canals.

'Umar abolished the Roman feudal system in Syria and gave lands to the cultivators, the actual tillers of the soil, and the revenue collected from Syria was 14,000,000 dīnārs.

In Persia from the time of the Sassanids the *takmilah* system was followed in the collection of land-tax. It consisted in assessing the *kharaj* in lump sums. In case the land was left uncultivated or some peasants escaped, the peasants remaining on the spot were liable to pay the entire amount. The old system continued under the Muslims. They themselves decided as to how much each individual cultivator was to pay and their burden was also

1. Baladhuri, pp. 24, 27, 29.
2. Abu Yusuf, p. 29
3. One *jarib* is equal to 3,600 sq. yards (60 cubits by 60 cubits).
4. Baladhuri, pp. 269, 271.
5. Quoted by al-Khudri, III, 143.

shared by craftsmen and other wage earners. The dues of defaulters was paid by the rest.[1] Contracts were made every fourth year and allowances were made every year for the making and repairing of dykes, and meeting draughts or other natural calamities at the rates specified in the registers of the *kharaj*. The Byzantines collected from the Copts an additional quantity of grains for provisioning the Roman soldiers. After conquest, the Muslims also collected this additional tax in the form of wheat, honey, oil, vinegar etc.[2] This was abolished by Hadrat 'Umar later. The average rate of tax was one *dīnar* and three *irdabs* (16½ bushels) of grain per *jarīb* and the annual revenue from Egypt was about 12,000,000 dīnārs.

Al-'Ushūr (*tithe*) was collected on the merchandise. On the report received from Abū Mūsa al-Ash'arī the Governor of Kūfah that the Muslim merchants trading in non-Muslim countries were paying 10% on their merchandise, 'Umar imposed 10% on non-Muslim merchants of *Dar al-Harab* (enemy country) trading in Muslim territory and 5% on the merchandise of the Dhimmis while Muslims were already paying 2½% on their merchandise. This they had to pay on goods worth not less than 200 dirhams.[3] Wood, seeds, grass and vegetables were exempt from 'Ushūr (*tithe*). The state share in the treasure trove was one-fifth.

The income from *al-Fayy'* lands increased generally. There were certain crown lands (*al-Fayy'*) like the estate of Fadak the income from which was spent on the Prophet's relatives, the orphans, the indigents, the wayfarers and on the general good of the Muslim community. During the time of the pious Caliphs all the lands belonging to fire temples, unclaimed lands and crown lands in the conquered countries were declared as *al-Fayy'* with their income amounting to 7,000,000 pieces.[4] Estates confiscated for active opposition to or rebellion against the Muslim State and forests, lands set apart for the construction of roads and the maintenance of postal service were included in *al-Fayy.'* 'Umar enunciated that land and money acquired in war constituted *Fayy'*

1. Maqrizi, *Khitat*, Vol. I, 77.
2. Baladhuri, 124-5, 152, 173-4, 179, 215
3. Abu Yusuf, p. 78
4. *Ibid.*, 22

and belonged to the Muslim community. Even after conversion to Islām peasants of *al-Fayy'* estates continued to pay land tax as usual. A good portion of *al-Fayy'* lands was assigned to the soldiers and converted to '*Ushri* lands later on. The income from State lands was spent on public works like digging of canals, construction of dams, dykes and tanks.

Public works:—There was no separate department for building and road construction, still under the instruction of 'Umar and the supervision of the provincial district officials, offices and residences for the officials were built. Among the public works mosques, inns. bridges and roads were constructed. Except treasury other constructions were of ordinary types. The treasury of Kūfah was constructed with the materials of the Persian buildings by a Majūsī mason named Ruzbah.[1] Special care was taken to construct a road between Madinah and Makkah and to make the journey between these two towns comfortable. At every stage (*manzil*, one day's *journey*) a police outpost, inns and wells were constructed.[2]

The Ka'bah was extended in 17H/638 A. D. and cover of Qubaṭi an Egyptian manufacture was used as *Ghilaf Ka'bah.* The Prophet's Mosque was extended from 100 yards to 140 yards and twenty yards it was extended in the width. Imams and mu'adhdhins were appointed in the mosques which were provided with lights and carpets from his time. The system of religious education was organised and paid preachers, teachers and jurists were appointed all over the conquered countries.

The *Khilafat* of Hadrat 'Umar is specially known for the foundation of Camp cities and development of villages into cities and construction of canals. In 14H/635 A. D. 'Utbah b. Ghazwān laid the foundation of Baṣrah and had it settled by 800 persons. It grew up so rapidly that by the time of the governorship of Ziyād b. Abū Sufyān the number of pensionholders of this city swelled to 80,000 and their family members to 120,000.

The ancient ruined capital of the 'Arab ruler Nu'mān b. Mundhir in 'Irāq was rebuilt and developed under the name of

1. Tabari, see Kufah
2. *Ibid.*, 2529.

Kūfah by Sa'd b. Abī Waqqās and residential houses were constructed for 40,000 persons. On the special instructions of 'Umar the main roads of this city were built twenty yards wide and streets thirty to forty-five feet. The Chief mosque was constructed for the congregational prayers of 40,000 persons.[1] A wide verandah of 100 yards long was built in front of the congregational hall. The town reached its glory during the time of 'Umar himself who called it *Ras Islam.* The twin cities of 'Irāq became known for literary and cultural activities and produced a number of renowned scholars.

On the conquest of Egypt 'Amr b. al-'Āṣ laid the foundation of Fusṭāt in a field between the Nile and the Mount Muqattam where he had pitched his tent originally from which the new city derived its name.[2] It developed rapidly and had the privilege of being the first 'Arab capital of Egypt. It was the wealth and pride of the West (al-Maghrib). Jazyah was another camp city in Egypt. After the conquest of Alexandria 'Amr b. al-'Āṣ posted a garrison on the sea-coast to guard the country against the Byzantine naval attacks. A fort was constructed there in 21 H/952 A.D. and thus a new town grew up there.

Mawṣil was originally a village but developed into a town by Harthamah b. 'Arfajah. It was called as such as it joined the East and the West.

Canals were dug for irrigating agricultural field and supplying sweet water to the villages and towns. The most important and useful canal was the *Nahr Amīr al-Mu'minīn* which connected the Nile and the Red Sea and made easy the transport of Egyptian goods to the Hijāz.[3] This was the monumental works of 'Umar al-Fārūq. A nine miles long canal called *Nahr Abī Mūsa* was dug to supply sweet water from the Euphrates to the Basrites.[4] Sa'd b. Abī Waqqāṣ, Governor of Kūfah, had a canal constructed which was named after him.[5] *Nahr Ma'qil* was dug from the

1. *Mu'jam al-Buldan,* VII, see Kufah
2. *Ibid.,* see Fustat.
3. Suyuti, *Husn al-Muhadarah,* 68
4. *Futuh al-Buldan,* 365
5. *Ibid.,* 383

Tigris reclaiming waste land and many irrigational canals were constructed in Khuzistān by al-Juz b. Mu'āwiyah. According to Maqrīzī 120,000 labourers were employed in digging canals in Egypt alone.[1]

Large meadows were set apart for grazing state animals from the time of Prophet Muḥammad. There were 400,000 camels and horses in the State pastures during the time of 'Umar.[2]

The Military Organization:—Prophet Muḥammad was not only the religious and civil head but also the military head of the Muslims. He himself marshalled the Muslim forces in all important battles and campaigns and sent detachments under *Amīr al-'Askar* (military commander) on small expeditions. He had no department for military affairs but he himself organised and looked after the welfare of the soldiers.[3]

On his arrival at Madīnah the Holy Prophet started the military organisation from a humble beginning for defence against the Makkans using the tribal tactics of *karr* and *farr* (strike and run). He had no standing army. For the battle of Badr he could raise only 313 volunteers against 1,000 well-armed and well-trained Makkan soldiers. In the battle he adopted the five winged formation (*ta'biyah*) arranging his men in straight regular ranks. The *saqah* (rearguard) had the charge of baggage, supplies and pack-animals. Pikemen protected by long shields were placed in the first row to await and receive the enemy attack and the archers were posted in the second line. In the battle of Siffīn. 'Alī arranged his infantry according to the *ṣaff* (straight line) method. In the battle of Badr the Prophet made the best use of his position and in the battle of the Ditch he adopted the Persian defensive tactics and protected the undefended part of the city by digging a ditch (*Khandaq*). In the hotly contested battle of Hunayn, Prophet Muḥammad adopted a simple stratagem and utilized the wind blowing towards the enemy by throwing dust and sand on the advanced detachments of the enemy. This blinded them and saved the Muslims from the first fury of their

1. Al-Maqrizi, I, 76
2. Baladhuri, 8, 9.
3. Ibn Hisham (edit Wustenfeld), I, 433, 454; Tabari, I, 319.

attack. In the siege of Tā'if, the Prophet employed *manjaniq* (ballista) and *dabbabah* (mantelet made of wood and hide).

The Prophet's successor Hadrat Abū Bakr proved his military genius in planning even larger expeditions, himself remaining at Madinah for subduing the entire sub-continent of Arabia in about a year's time.

After the conquest of Persia, Syria and Egypt when the 'Arab Empire extended extensively, it became difficult to divide the State's income among all the units of the army without keeping any record. Further 'Umar thought of making gradations between the old and new converts. Therefore, in order to regulate the receipts and disbursement of the revenue, he established a *Dīwan* (Finance Department). After disbursing the expenditure of the revenue collection and civil administration and meeting the military requirements the surplus was spent on the community. A register was maintained of all 'Arab and their *mawalī* (non-Arab Muslim) pension-holders. The widow of the Prophet Hadrat 'Ai'shah receiving 12,000 dirhams annually topped the stipend list.[1] Persons who had participated in the battle of Badr were given a pension of 5,000 dirhams each. The same amount was given to the Prophet's uncle, 'Abbās, and his two grandsons. Hasan and Husayn.[2] The sons of the warriors of Badr and those who accepted Islām after the conquest of Makkah were given 2,000 dirhams each. Those who accepted Islām before the migration to Abyssinia were allowed 4,000 dirhams each and those who had embraced Islām before the conquest of Makkah received 3,000 each. Theologians and others who had rendered special services to Islām were given high pensions.[3] The 'Arab soldiers and their *mawalī* received 400 dirhams each.[4] The wives and children of the soldiers who had fallen in battle or were in active service were assigned 100 dirhams. Every Muslim child received an annuity and as he grew up his annuity increased. The slaves also received annuities equal to their masters. There

---

1. Abu Yusuf, 25
2. *Ibid.*, 25
3. *Ibid.*, 25
4. *Ibid.*

were separate registers for the regular and standing army and for those who could be called in for active service.

Non-'Arab Muslims who were given secondary position in Muslim society were kept in reserve to help the fighting Muslim soldiers when so required. The intelligence officers were recruited generally from among the non-Muslims. A Jew named Yūsuf served as such in the siege of Qasāriyah.[1] The Magians supplied information about the enemy movements in 'Irāq. Many Magians joined Muslim force as members of volunteer corps and received regular salaries. Four thousand Daylamites, who had joined Yazdgird's army, joined the Muslims after the battle of Qādisiyah. They were separately registered. Many Indian Jats who were settled in 'Irāq and served in the Persian army accepted Islām and received annuities.

This was the first attempt made in the history of the world for the State to take upon itself the collective responsibility for the supply of food and clothing to the entire population. Even a critic like Muir did not fail to appreciate 'Umar's introduction of the Dīwān. "A great nation dividing amongst them their whole revenues, spoils and conquests, first on the principle of equal brotherhood, and next on that of martial merit and spiritual distinction, is a spectacle probably without parallel in the world."[2] This preserved the identity of the 'Arabs who then numbered only about 150,000 and saved them from being absorbed in the more populous conquered countries. The system of paying regular salaries to the soldiers attached them to the rulers directly unlike the Byzantine and Persian soldiers who were attached to the landlords since the feudal military system was prevalent in Syria and Persia. But as this system combined military and civil pensions into one it could not work for long.

With a view to organize the Muslim 'Arabs into a martial aristocracy 'Umar did not allow them to acquire lands outside Arabia or to settle with non-Muslims in their towns. Accordingly military camps were opened in the countries. There were five camps in Syria, one in Palestine, two in 'Irāq and two in Egypt

1. *Futuh al-Buldan*, 148
2. Muir, *Annals of Early Caliphate*, 227.

viz., al-Jabiyah, Hims, Amwās, Tabariyah and al-Ludd (Lydda) in Syria, Ramlah in Palestine, Kūfah and Baṣrah in 'Irāq and Fusṭāṭ and Jazyah in Egypt.

There were regular well-ventilated barracks for soldiers and huge stables for about 40,000 horses, and a record office and provision store in each camp. The horses were branded on their haunches, 'Fighter in the way of God' *Jaysh fī sabīl Allah*).[1] Special arrangement was made for breeding superior varieties of horses. There were also military barracks in big cities and at strategic positions.

Attached to each military station was *al-'Arīf* (the pay master) to disburse salaries. Every tribe had an 'Arīf and he received 100,000 dirhams which he distributed among his soldiers through his subordinate officers. There were a hundred '*Arīfs* in Kūfah and Baṣrah through whom 10,000,000 dirhams were distributed. The officers were paid 7,000 to 10,000 dirhams and the soldiers 200 dirhams annually. Subsequently each soldier's emolument was raised to 300 dirhams. Soldiers on active service received also free rations, dress, medical aid etc. and their wives and children drew pensions from the treasury. Besides this regular income they had their shares in the four-fifths of the booty.[2] Often the emoluments of the soldiery were increased in appreciation of their services. Thus the salaries of the warriors of Qādisiyah namely Zahrah, 'Asma, Dabi etc. were increased from 2,000 to 2,500 dirhams.

Swimming, horse-riding, artillery practice and barefooted marching were among the items of compulsory training. Soldiers had to live hard lives. During marches, soldiers had their weekly rest on Fridays and after every four months of active service they were allowed leave to go to their houses.[3] Special care was taken for maintaining sound health of the soldiers and assuring their comforts expeditions were sent to hot countries in winter and to cold countries in summer.

Soldiers were graded into units of tens, hundreds and

---

1. *Kanz al-'Ummal*, II, 231
2. Tabari, I, 2204-5
3. Abu Da'ud, *Kitab al-Kharaj*, Chapter on soldiery.

thousands. The officer-in-charge of ten soldiers was *Amīr al-Ashrah* (*decurion*), that of the hundred, *al-Qa'id* (lieutenant) and that of thousand, *Amīr* (commander). The army was consisted of *al-rijal* (infantry), *al-fursan* (the cavalry), *al-rumal* (the archers), *al-ghilam* (service corps), *al-tabi'ah* (scouts) and *al-rid* (rear-scouts). The system of maintaining a bodyguard was instituted by the Governor of Syria, Mu'āwiyah. It was his bodyguard who saved him from the fierce attack of Malik al-Ashtar in the battle field of Siffīn.

Against Syria and Persia the entire 'Arab race had been mobilised, although the 'Arab armies were always inferior to them in numbers. There were 4,000 soldiers in Kūfah.[1] According to Ibn Sa'd every year 3,000 new soldiers were recruited.[2] About 10,000 soldiers were kept ready for war. In the battle of Siffīn 'Alī mustered 90,000 and Mu'āwiyah 85,000.[3]

Among the weapons that the Muslim soldiers used were swords mostly double-edged,[4] lauces, bows and arrows smaller in size than the Persian ones[6] and slings. Coats of mail being costly were seldom used. Shields and helmets were the arms of protection. Mantelets (wooden *dabbabah*), catapults (ballistas) and hole-makers (*naqqabun*) were used to attack forts and towns. Barricades and ditches were used in defending the camps andcities.

The army marched in battle order, the scouts marehing ahead of the vanguard reconnoitring and rear scouts following the rearguard. Bag and baggage, women and children, sick and wounded, flocks and herds moved with the rearguard.

Al-ra'id, an officer, was appointed to choose a suitable place for encampment. The camp in the enemy country was protected by a fire ditch and barricades and was guarded by sentries.

In the beginning the 'Arab army did not have any organised system of supply. The supplies of necessary articles for the army were later regularised by opening *Ahra* (the Army Supply Department) and 'Umar appointed 'Āmir b. 'Utbah to organise it.

1. Tabari, I, 2850; *al-Faruq* (Urdu), I, Lahore, 348
2. Tabari, I, 2850
3. Al-Mas'udi, IV, 344
4. Baladhuri, 55
5. *Ibid.*, 55.

The waving of flags served the purpose of alarm bells and signals in the battlefield. The first wave meant a break-up for attending calls of nature and offering prayers etc., the second wave indicated an alert and the third was the signal for a solid attack on the enemy. It is recorded that the Muslim general Nu'mān used flags for giving such signals.[1]

In organisation, supplies, weapons, technical skill, tactics and in morale the Muslims surpassed the Persians and the Byzantines and proved their worth by achieving victories against huge armies with lesser numbers. The Muslims won several battles because of their great valour and superior tactics.

In the battle of *Walijah*, Khālid threw his reserve soldiers kept in ambush at the critical moment of the battle and won it. As substitutes for helmets[2] Muslim soldiers bound leather thongs round their heads and charged the enemy at close quarter with their lances and swords in the battle of Qādisiyah. The Muslims took courage in their fight against the Persian elephants and cut off their trunks and the girdles of their howdas frightening the animals and killing their riders who toppled down. In order to frighten the horses of the enemy, they covered their camels with white blankets and led them against the enemies. As the occasion demanded the Muslims put their resources in men and armour and drew the advantages of the fighting position to the best of their utility. Khālid won the battle of Yarmūk against the Byzantines by re-arranging his troops in thirty-eight *Kurdus* (cohorts) of more than one thousand each and attacking the enemy from two sides and pressing the attack from the centre.[3] At close quarters the 'Arab horsemen set aside their bows and arrows and used swords. In short it was because of their military genius, discipline studed with their religious faith the Muslims conquered so many countries despite the superiority of their enemies in numbers, arms and equipment.[4]

1. Baladhuri, 55
2. Levy, *Sociology of Islam,* II, 303
3. Tabari, I, 2093; *al-Khudri,* I, 276-8.
4. cf. *A Political History of the Muslims,* Vol. I *(Prophet and Pious Caliphs)* Dacca, 1970, pp. 227-258.

CHAPTER II

ADMINISTRATION

UNDER THE UMAYYADS AND THE ABBASIDS

Khalifah: – As *Amīral-Mu'minīn* the *Khalifah* described himself as such on coins, led the pilgrims to Hajj, read the *Khutbah* in his own name on Friday from the pulpit of the Jami' Mosque claiming from his Muslim subjects some of the reverences paid by them to Prophet Muḥammad. Although in his own case as a democrat Mu'awiyah preferred consensus of opinion to the Kingship discarding 'Ali,[1] yet he became ambitious to perpetuate the Cliphate in his own family[2] by nominating his son Yazid as his successor and by obtaining *ba'yt* (oath of allegiance) from the chiefs of Syria and 'Irāq for him and by taking him to Makkah and Madīnah to have forced oath of allegiance to him from the citizens of the two holy cities.

With 'Ali, the first period of *Khilafat* ended (661 A.D.) and that of the second began initiated by Mu'āwiyah. He was the first in Islam to introduce the principle of dynastic and hereditary *Khilafat*. Mu'āwiyah held that in a democratic system the stability of a government could not be maintained and as he apprehended war between the Umayyads and the Hashimids, after his death, he thought of continuing the *Khilafat* in his own line by nominating his son Yazīd as *Walī-'ahd* (successor). He tried to preserve the system of election in the form of *ba'yh* the ceremony by which the chiefs laid their hands on that of the new Caliph as a sign of homage. *Ba'yt* was taken in the provinces at the hands of the governors and other officials on behalf of Yazīd.[3] Under the influence of the Romans and the Persians and on the advice of Mughīrah b. Shu'bah, Mu'āwiyah thus introduced the hereditary principle of *Khilafat*. Husayn b. 'Alī and 'Abd Allāh

---

1. cf. Ibn Qutaybah, *'Uyun al-Akhbar*, Berlin 1900-8, p. 22
2. Tabari, II, pp. 176-7.
3. Author's *A Political History of the Muslims*, Vol. II, pp. 11-12.

b. Zubayr established themselves as rival Caliphs, one after the other, at Kūfah and Makkah respectively. Husayn met his martyrdom at Karbala but 'Abd Allāh's *Khilafat* was accepted in the Hijāz and Egypt. It was the fourth Caliph of the Umayyad dynasty, namely 'Abd al-Malik who got 'Abd Allāh ibn Zubayr killed by Hajjāj b. Yūsuf in the battle of Makkah in Oct. 692[1] and established his rule over all the Muslim territories. Before that by constructing the *Qubbat al-Sakhrah* (Dome of the Rock) at Jerusalem, he had tried to divert the attention of the Muslims from Makkah to Jerusalem. Thus the hereditary system of succession in which a son or a brother, on the basis of seniority or ability, used to be nominated by the dying caliph was established and this continued throughout the *Khilafat* of the Umayyads and the Abbasids. Although in practice the *Khilafat* passed from father to son or brother to brother the office in theory continued to be elective through *ba'yt* system. The Sufyanid Umayyads nominated one candidate for the *Khilafat* while the Marwanid Umayyads nominated two candidates for the same to succeed one another. The *Khilafat* was thus changed into a *Mulk* (Kingship). Marwān nominated his two sons, 'Abd al-Malik and 'Abd al-'Azīz, to succeed him, one after the other. 'Abd al-'Azīz died before 'Abd al-Malik so the latter nominated two of his sons al-Walīd and Sulaymān and the latter, in turn, nominated a cousin and a brother, namely, 'Umar b. 'Abd al-'Azīz and Yazīd b. 'Abd al-Malik following the principle of nominating two grown up persons. Yazīd II nominated his brother Hishām in preference to his minor son Walīd as his successor and the latter to succeed Hishām.

After taking the oath of fealty at the hands of one or two successors the Ca iph handed over the document to the nominated son or brother or his representative. This nomination paper was kept in the treasury, Chief Mosque or Ka'bah or with a trustee.

The basis of the government was no more to be found in popular support as it had been under the two early Caliphs. It was now to be found in diplomacy and the dynasty was supported like 'Amr ibn al-'Āṣ, Zayd ibn 'Alī b. Mughirah ibn Shu'bah,

1. Tabari, II, 852.

Hajjāj b. Yūsuf and others. Unlike the Pious Caliphs the Umayyads became truly Kings secular in character although in their early days they had chiefs as *primus interpares.* A feudal society was growing from a tribal one and it required feudal over-lordship. The Umayyads who were free disposer of the *fayy* land of the Muslims supplied them with it.

The Khalīfah being secular and religious head of the faithful Muslims was bound to abide by the rules and regulations framed on customs if not contrary to the religious principles of Islam. The first two Caliphs consulted the most important leaders of Islam but from the time of the third Caliph Hadrat 'Uthmān not much importance was attached to the Shūrā. During the time of Mu'āwiyah the Shūrā consist of a few topmost men was more or less a council of Elders of the Umayyad Chiefs only. 'Umar II reorganised the Shūrā and both during the period of his governorship of Hijāz and Khilāfat of Damascus he consulted a council of advisers. To discuss and decide important questions the decision of the Shūrā was accepted though not practised by Umayyad Caliphs. While Hadrat 'Uthman started the practice of disposing off the *fayy' lands* of the Muslims and bestowing gifts lavishly, Mu'āwiyah completed the process. During his rule the stipends of many persons were discontinued or reduced and the names of many new ones were inserted in the register. This gave Mu'āwiyah absolute power. He instituted the system of body guard (*al-haras*) and constructed a *maqsurah* in the mosque for his personal security and sat on a throne.[2] 'Umar was a *mab'ūth*, the expected saint, after a century. He tried to simplify the pompous life of the Umayyads by wearing patched clothes, taking simple food from the public kitchen and sitting on floor like his grandfather 'Umar I. He mixed so freely with the people[2] that it was difficult for a stranger to distinguish him as a Caliph, but soon after his death the grand court of the Umayyads was revised Thus the *Khalīfah* became more a political head than a religious one destroying much of the religious halo attached to his person and sanctity attached to his caliphal office.

1. cf. Ibn Khaldun, I, p. 217
2. Ibn al-Jawzi, pp. 173-4, 145.

The Abbasids started a movement for revival of an impartial State of the early Muslims where men like Salmān of Fars, Bilāl of Abyssinia and a prince like Ibn Jabalah could have equal rights in protest against the worldliness of the Umayyads. The Abbasid dynasty claimed itself to be *dawlah* (a revolutionary State) and indeed it departed from the Umayyad dynasty in many ways. The ascendancy of the Arabs was over and while the Khurāsānis became the Caliphal body-guards the Persians occupied the Key positions in the Government, a new hierarchy of officers other than that of the Arabs grew. Their temporal hold on distant provinces loosened although spiritual authority remained. Special stress was laid on the religious character of the State, possession of and reverence to the Holy cities of Makkah and Madinah, wearing of Prophet's mantle and holding of his staff in hand by the Caliphs represented the 'Arab Shaykhs while the Abbasid Caliphs represented the Persian monarchs. Rank and dignity ceased to be hereditary and depended on the whims and fancies of the Caliph. The actual work of administration was left in the hands of the Wazīr, the Caliph, however, remained the sole arbiter of the life and death of the subjects.

While leading members of the royal family formed a sort of council under the Umayyads, besides the royal family members the members of loyal families like the Barmakids were also included in the council of the Khilāfat under the early Abbasids. Al-Ma'mūn constituted a regular council of state which continued under the later Abbasids and even in the principalities after the break up of the Abbasid Empire. On the fall of the Umayyad Caliphate at Damascus (750 A.D.) while Abbasid Caliphate (750-1258) was founded first at Kufah and then at Baghdad an Umayyad Amirate (756-929) followed by an Umayyad Caliphate (929-1031) was established at Cordova and a Shi'ite Fatimid Caliphate (909-1171) grew up first at Mahdiyah and then at Cairo. The Umayyads in Spain and the Fatimids in Egypt also followed hereditary system of *Khilafat*.

The hereditary principle of succession introduced by the Umayyads was followed by the Abbasid Caliphs with the same evil results. Thus the reigning Caliph nominated as his successor one of his sons or kinsman whom he favoured or considered best suited for the *Khilafat*. Of the first twenty-four Abbasid Caliphs (750-991) only six were immediately succeeded by a son, others were brothers or other kinsmen. Al-Saffāḥ designated his brother al-Manṣūr and al-Hādī was succeeded by his brother Hārūn who nominated his younger son, al-Amīn, as his first successor, and his elder son Ma'mūn although comparatively more efficient as his second successor. Ma'mūn ignoring his son al-'Abbās nominated his brother al-Mu'taṣim. Ma'mūn al-Rashīd held the Shi'ah view of Divine *Imamat* and that leadership passed from Prophet Muḥammad to Hadrat 'Alī and vested in some members of the house of 'Alī and hence Ma'mūn thought of nominating 'Alī b. Mūsā b. Ja'far al-Sādiq a descendant of Hadrat' Alī as his successor with the title of Ridā. He was dissuaded by the Abbasid supporters from doing this and forced to re-introduce the hereditary principle of successions.

The early Abbasid Caliphs succeeded in evolving a unique administrative structure. The state activities were entrusted to various administrative departments with functions clearly defined. At the helm of affairs was the Caliph as a supreme ruler with unlimited authority over the State. Although the Abbasid Caliph exercised religious authority as *Imam* he had civil authority, judicial power and military function as temporal head of the State.

The ascendancy of the Abbasid dynasty of the Calipaate meant that the centre of gravity of the Islamic empire was shifted from the zone of 'Arab influence to that of the Persians i.e. Damascus to Baghdād. Under the 'Abbasids the traditions of the Persian monarchy reasserted themselves and the Abbasid caliphs sat on throne in solemn majesty surrounded by their guards and the executioner stood with drawn swords by their sides. At the same time the Abbasids laid emphasis on the religious aspect of the *Khilafat* wearing *burdah* (mantle) of the Prophet[1] and functioning as protectors of Islam and created awe in the eyes of the devout Muslims by elaborating the court of etiquette.

---

1. De Goeje, *Fragmente Historicorum Arabicorum*, I, pp. 82, 208 quoted by Levy, *The Social Structure of Islam*, Cambridge 1957, p. 293n4.

Although the Caliph was the final arbiter of all government affairs he delegated his civil powerr to the *Wazīr*, judicial authority to the *Qadi al-Qudat* and military functions to the *Amīr* (commander-in-chief). Delegating authority to the *Wazir* Manṣūr and Mahdi kept control over the administration. The early and competent Abbasid Caliphs appointed wazirs and heads of the *Dīwans* and sometimes they made *wazīr* in charge of one or more *dīwans* also as under Mahdī.[1] On appointing Ya'qūb ibn Dā'ūd as his wazīr Mahdī accepted 100,000 dinars from him.[2]

From the 9th century the 'Abbasid Caliphs began to lose direct control over the government and consequently the delegation of power to the *Wazīr* and other government officials increased. With the decline of their temporal power emphasis was laid on the religious leadership (*Imamat*) of the Caliphs. By 946 A.D. all effective power had passed out of the hands of the *Khilafat*.

Drawing lessons from the Umayyads, the Abbasids had laid emphasis on his religious leadership and the more the Caliph became weak and figure-head a century after the establishment of the Abbasids the more honorific titles of *Khalīfah* (the Vicegerent of God) and *Dhil Allah 'ala al-Ard* (God's shadow on earth) were conferred on him by the subjects in lieu of *Khalifahtu Rasulillah* (the Vicegerent of the Messenger of God) conferred on him early.[3] Al-Mutawakkil (847-61) was the first to receive such titles.

During the decaying period of the Abbasids, the Caliphs were mere puppets in the hands of the *Amir al-Umara'*, the Buwayhids and the Saljuqs, and were removed from the office as the courtiers desired.[4] On the fall of the Abbasids in 1258 at the hands of Hulāgū Khān, the Caliphate was transferred from Baghdād to Cairo three years after in 1261 under the Mamluks. Al-Musta'sim's uncle al-Mustanṣir[5] was installed as Caliph at Cairo by the fourth Mamluk ruler al-Zahir al-Malik Baybars (1260-77). From Cairo it passed on to Constantinople in January

1. Jahshiyari, pp. 81, 84
2. Al-Fakhri, p. 219
3. Al-Mas'udi, VII, 278
4. cf. Ibn Khaldun, *Prolegomenes*, tr. de Slane, I, pp. 392-96; Mawardi, p. 25
5. Abu'l-Fida', III, p. 222.

1517 and from the hands of the Qurays͟h to those of the Ottomans, Salīm I[1] being the first and Sultān Caliph, Muḥammad VI, the last and 'Abd al-Majīd the last Caliph without the sultanate. Finally the Caliphate was abolished by Mustafa Kamal Ataturk in March 1924.

In practice all the Caliphs before the Ottoman ruler Salim I were from the Qurays͟h. None from the non-Qurays͟h ever claimed the K͟hilāfat. Even when the Abbasid Caliphs became unable to rule themselves their religious rights were not usurped by the secular heads like the Buwayhid, Saljūq and G͟haznawid Sultans in whose hands they were puppets or Sultan Salāḥuddin Ayyūbī who had full control over al-'Adid (1160-71) the last Fatimid Caliph on whose dethronement he read the *Kbutbah* in the name of the Abbasid Caliph Mustadi' in 1171.[2] On the conquest of Egypt Salīm I took the puppet Abbasid Caliph Mutawakkil prisoner to Turkey and assumed himself the K͟hilāfat. Salīm's son and successor Sulaymān the Magnificent sent Mutawakkil to Egypt to live a retired life and finally to die there in 1543.[3] This was the first time that the *Khilafat* was transferred from the Qurays͟h to the non-Qurays͟h Turk which act is justified by the Hanafī theologians.

On gathering experience from the workings of the Caliphate at Damascus, Bag͟hdād, Cairo and Cordova treatises were written on Muslim administration defining the qualifications, privileges and functions of a Caliph. The Sunnite writers like al-Māwardī (d. 1058), al-Wasafi (d. 1310) and Ibn K͟haldūn (d. 1406) analysed the qualifications of a Caliph thus : a Qurays͟h, male and adult, sound of mind and body, competent to defend the faith and country and qualified to command respect and reverence of the Muslims.[4] To legalize the Turkish *Khilafat*, later jurists changed the word Qurays͟h with Muslim having all other qualifications as before.

At the time of oath taking ceremony under the Abbasids *Mir Munshī* called the persons to take oath and *Wazīr* or his deputy bound a turban round the head of the Caliph and put a

1. cf. *Mas'udi, Muruj al-Dhahab,* VII, p. 278.
2. Abu al-Fida, Vol. III, 47; Ibn Khallikan, Vol. I, pp. 405-7; Yaqut, II, pp. 246-7
3. Abu al-Fida', Vol. III, 53; cf. Zaydan, *Ta'rikh-i -Tamaddun Islam,* p. 151.
4. cf. Hitti, P.K.-*History of the Arabs,* 1953 p. 705

wrapper on his body.[1] The Amīr, military officer, and the Qādī of Baghdad were the first to take oath. Towards the end of the ceremony a number of titles were offered and the Caliph used to choose any one of them. In the beginning the titles used to be simple like *Rashīd, Amīn, Ma'mūn* but later they became cumbrous and showy as *al-Mu'tasim bi'llah.* At the end the throne of Caliphate with valuable presents were offered to him. Riding on horse back and accompained by courtiers the Caliph in pomp and grandeur proceeded to the *Dīwan al-'Ām* and a soldier walked with an unsheathed sword in hand infront of the Caliph's horse. After sitting on the throne in the *Dīwan al-'Ām* he received the delegations coming from provinces and districts. The wordings of oath-taking ceremony were simple and short during the time of the early Caliphs and were recited orally. Later wordings became cumbrous and complex and increased gradually to the size of three pages in writing during the time of *Khalīfah* 'Amr bi'llah 'Abbasi in the eighth century of Hijri era.[2]

Prophet's silver seal with the inscription *Muḥammad Rasūl Allah* was used by the early three Caliphs until it fell into the well of the Umayyads and the Abbasids had their own independent seal with phrases having similarity with their names. Mu'āwiyah introduced wax in sealing after being cheated once by 'Umar bin Zubayr. The seal of Mā'mūn read as *'Abd Allah Yaumin bi'llah*, of Wathq as *Allahu Thaqqat a-l-Wathiq* and of Mutawakkil as *Ala' Allahu tawakkaltu.*[3]

The administration in general at the centre and in the provinces is now being discussed here under two heads, the Umayyads and the Abbasids, the first being the formative period and the second that of development.

1. Prophet Muhammad had given a wrapper to an 'Arab poet, Ka'b b. Zubayr ibn Abi Salman, from whose family it was purchased by Mu'awiyah for 40,000 dirhams and held by the Umayyads and Abbasids until it was acquired by Salim I on the conquest of Egypt in 1517 A.D. It was not taken away by the Mongols on the fall of Baghdad in 1258 as presumed by Abu'l-Fida. It is preserved in the old Sarai of Istanbul. (Zaydan, p. 162).
2. Zaydan, pp. 159-160
3. *Ibid.*, p p. 162-164.

SECTION I

UMAYYAD ADMINISTRATION

To assist the Caliph in administration there were six Boards at the Centre : *Dīwan al-Kharaj* (the Board of Revenue), *Dīwan al-Rasa'il* (the Board of Correspondence), *Dīwan al-Khatam* (the Board of Signet), *Dīwan al-Barīd* (the Board of Posts), *Dīwan al-Qada* (Board of Justice) and *Dīwan al-Jund* (the Military Board)

Dīwan al-Kharaj :-- The Central Board of Revenue adminstered the entire finance of the empire, it imposed and collected taxes and disbursed revenue. It also directly administered the revenue side *al-Sawad* the richest region of the Empire. While *Dīwan al-Kharaj* dealt with Public lands and revenue there was *Dīwan al-Mustaghallat* to receive rents for the use of State lands and property.

Fiscal Reforms :—In principle all Muslims expected equal facilities from the State. On expansion of the Islamic State many non-'Arabs started accepting Islam particularly in al-'Iraq and Khurāsān, leaving the villages for the cities with the hope to join the army as mawālī (clients) as according to Muslim law the Muslims were to pay hitherto *Zakat* (poor rate) only, but for any land they paid either no tax or used to pay tax at reduced rate *al-'ushr* (one-tenth). On conversion their taxes were reduced, they were obliged to pay *zakat* only and on becoming soldiers received a special subsidy. As a result the State suffered doubly, income reduced and expenditure in the form of stipends increased. To restore the economic condition 'Abd al-Malik in consultation with Hajjāj b. Yūsuf took measures to send the newly converted Muslims back to their farms in the villages[1] and pay their usual taxes which they paid before conversion e.g. *Kharaj* (land tax) and *Jīzyah* (poll-tax)

Kharaj was originally used in a loose sense tribute or tax realized from non-Muslims and was synonymous to *jizyah*. It was only by the end of the first century of the Hijri era

1. Mubarrad, p. 286.

used strictly for land tax and *jizyah* began to be used as poll-tax only. Hence even the 'Arab Muslims acquiring landed property in a *Kharaj* territory were asked by Hajjaj b. Yūsuf to pay the usual tax on the land they held. Although a purely administrative measure undertaken to save the State from bankruptcy yet the payment of these taxes were resented very much by the *Mawalis* (neo-Muslims). Moreover the neo-Muslims in Khurāsān became dissatisfied with the harsh administration of their governor, Yazīd b. Muhallab. To meet their grievances, as a pious Muslim, the Caliph 'Umar b. 'Abd al-'Āzīz (717-20) reverted to the policy adopted by his namesake 'Umar b. al-Khattāb and announced that these Khurāsānī *Mawalī* Muslims must be placed on an equal footing with the 'Arab Muslims by imposing only one tax namely *zakat* on them. *Zakat* was levied only on annual savings of a Muslim after defraying all his expenses, if he saved more than 200 *dirhams.* While distributing the pensions *zakat* was deducted by Mu'āwiyah from the pensioners due for the year.[1] That 'Umar's main interest lay more in the spread of Islam than in mere collection of revenue is evident from his reply to a complaint made by an Egyptian official that conversion was seriously affecting the treasury. 'Umar said "God sent His Prophet as a missionary, not as a tax-gatherer."

'Umar's leniency in collection provided great incentive for conversion and many Persians and Berbers accepted Islam to enjoy the consequent pecuniary privileges diminishing the revenue of the State greatly. To check this 'Umar b. 'Abd al-'Aziz propounded an agreement with the '*Ulama*' in Madīnah and declared that as *Kharaj* land was the joint property of the Muslim community it could not be broken up and transformed by sale to Muslims into their private property. Like 'Umar I, he, therefore, prohibited the sale of *Kharaj* lands to Muslims by issuing an edict after 100/718-9. Since then the *Kharaj* land on its owner's acceptance of Islam reverted to the village community.[2]

1. Hitti, p. 225; Khuda Bakhsh, *Orient under the Caliphs*, p. 187; Husaini, p. 128
2. Ibn al-Jawzi, *Sirat 'Umar ibn 'Abd al-'Aziz*, Cairo, 1331, pp. 88-9; Ya'qubi, 362, ibn Sa'd, V, pp. 277; Wellhausen, pp. 280-81; *Orient under the Caliphs*, p. 209.

or he continued to use it as a leaseholder. Exemption from land revenue induced the farmers of Transoxiana to accept Islam in large number. On the protests made by revenue officials and *dihqans* (village chiefs) the governor of Khurasan, Asad ibn 'Abdu'l-lah re-imposed the *Kharaj* on the Muslims.[1] Naṣr b. Sayyar al-Laythi (d. 131/748) the governor of Khurāsān (comprising Merw, Nisabur, Merw al-Rudh and Harat) under Hisham regulated the relations between the neo-Mus ims and the *Dhimmis* by ordaining that all land owners, including Muslims, would pay the *Kharaj* (land-tax) while *jizyah* (poll-tax) should be paid by the *Dhimmis* exclusively.[2]

In spite of the modifications introduced 'Umar's system did not continue as the state revenue was diminished and the number of clients (*Mawali*) had increased in the town paralysing the economy of the state.[3] With minor modifications the system of Hajjāj bin Yūsuf was re-introduced by latter Umayyad rulers drawing a clear cut distinction between *jizyah* and *kharaj*. Under the revised system the treasury continued to receive its main income from *kharaj* paid by the *Dhimmis* as well as the Muslims.

Khurāsān being an area of '*ahdi* land, the Muslims did not meddle in its revenue administration and the natives were to pay a fixed amount of tribute. According to the settlement the natives collected this amount from the general masses under two heads partly poll-tax (*jizyah*) and partly land-tax (*kharaj*). According to Muslim law the conversion to Islam freed the Mawali from the payment of poll-tax and not from land-tax. In other provinces 'Umar II's edict was followed and Mawalis were not required to pay *jizyah*. The Khurasani chiefs had also been ordered to exempt the Mawali from the payment of *jizyah* but, instead of paying heed to this, the native chiefs collected taxes at a higher rate from the Muslims and exempted their own men or collected taxes from them at a reduced rate. An enquiry board appointed by Naṣr bin Sayyār, Governor of Khurāsān, found on investigation that 30,000 Mawāli paid *jizyah* and 80,000 natives were exempt

1. Levy, *Sociology of Islam*, I, p, 34
2. cf. *Encyclopaedia of Islam*, article on Nasr b. Sayyar.
3. Ibn al-Jawzi, pp. 99-100; Hitti, p. 219; cf. Husaini, p. 133.

from poll-tax.[1] Accordingly Naṣr b. Sayyār had strictly prohibited the collection of *jizyah* from the Mawāli. The land was classified and land-tax was reassessed and levied on all equally irrespective of their creed and religion. Thus removing the abuses prevailing in the revenue organisation Naṣr bin Sayyar reformed the revenue system. The Umayyads did not survive long to draw benefit from his revenue reform which has helped in the augmentation of the treasury but it proved beneficial to the Abbasids.

Throughout the Umayyad period believers as well as unbelievers were made to pay land tax (Kharāj). Because of the conversion of a large number of the 'Irāqis the revenue of the country was reduced from a hundred million *dīnars* under 'Umar b. al-Khattāb to forty million under 'Abd al-Malik[2] and that of Egypt from fourteen million in the governorship of 'Amr ibn al-'Āṣ to five million in the time of Mu'āwiyah and later to four million under Hārūn al-Rashīd the 'Abbāsid Caliph (786-809).[3] One of the main causes for the decline of State revenae was undoubtedly the increase of the neo-Muslims in the towns and for the fall of the Umayyads the dissatisfaction of the non-'Arab Muslims and their joining to the cause of the Shi'ites in 'Irāq and to that of the Khārjites in Persia and Ifriqiyah.

Fayy'-Land :—At the time of conquering lands outside Arabia if resistance was made by the enemies, they were defeated by force and their properties were acquired. Except landed property the moveable ones formed the part of *ghanīmah* and distributed among the recipients. The landed property, however, formed part of state land and was declared as *Fayy* land and its income (*kharaj*) was to be distributed like booty and the *fayy'* land became the community property. Such state acquired lands were to be applied not for the advantage of the generation then living but as *fayy* belonging to the whole community for the benefit of all future generations of Muslim also. Later when agricultural reforms took place those inhabitants who cultivated *fayy'* land

1. cf. Al-Fakhri, pp. 215-6; Tabari, III, 1030.
2. Ya'qubi, *Kitab al-Buldan*, Leyden, 1892, II, 277; Arnold, T. W., *The Preaching of Islam*, London 1913, p. 81
3. Ya'qubi, p. 339.

and adopted Islām were asked to pay the *Kharaj* to Muslim treasury. There was no *fayy'* land in *Dar al-Sulh*, those districts whose inhabitants had voluntarily surrendered on the approach of the Muslim army agreeing to pay the *Kharaj* or tribute. The land in the conquered provinces, however, ceased to be regarded as *fayy* because on adopting Islām the owners of these *fayy* lands began, in spite of all measures of the Muslim authorities, to avoid the payment of *Kharaj* and paid like the 'Arab Muslims only the *zakat* (*'ushr*) on the yield of their fields. According to the views of later Muslim jurists *Kharaj*, *jizyah* and other taxes paid by non-Muslims were also included in *fayy'*.

As Hajjāj b. Yūsuf tried to replenish the Umayyad treasury he also tried to develop agricultural farms. A number of new canals were dug besides restoration of the large ones between the Euphrates and the Tigris. Uncultivated plots of land were tilled and the submerged ones were drained.

Development of agriculture and other economic resources in the provinces undertaken by the Umayyads resulted in the overflow of revenue in the central exchequer. The revenue from 'Irāq under 'Umar I dwindled to one third when 'Abd al-Malik succeeded e.g., from 120,000,000 to 40,000,000 *dirhams*. It was again raised to 130,000,000 *dirhams* per annum. The annual revenue from Egypt was 3,099,000 *dīnars* or 36,000,000 *dirhams*.[1] It amounted to 20,000,000 *dirhams* from Syria[2] and 6,000,000 *dirhams* from Sindh per year.

Dīwan al-Rasa'il:—A regular Board of Correspondence was established under the Umayyads. It issued state missives and circulars to the Central and Provincial Officers. It co-ordinated the work of all Boards and dealt with all correspondence as the chief secretariate. Al-Jahshiyārī has preserved some of these documents in his book *Kitab al-Wuzara,' wa'l-Kuttab*. A *Katib* of Marwān II namely 'Abd al-Hamid introduced a very flowery style with polite phraseology[3] which was followed and improved upon later under the 'Abbasids particularly by Rukn al-Dawlah's wazīr Ibn al-'Amīd.

1. Jurji Zaydan, *Ta'rikh al-Tamaddun al-Islam*, II (Urdu tr.), Karachi, p. 27.
2. *Ibid.*,
3. Mas'udi, VI, p. 81; Ibn Khallikan, I, 550.

Registers :—Nationalization of the State began with the changing of the language of the *Dīwan* (Public registers) from Greek to Arabic at the Umayyad capital, Damascus, and from Pahlawī to Arabic in the eastern provinces and from Greek and Latin to Arabic in the western viceroyalty under Khalifahs 'Abd al-Malik and al-Walīd and with the creation of the Arabic coinage.

At the outset under the orthodox caliphs local administration was disturbed little and the old system of maintaining registers and circulation of coinage were retained in the provinces with little modifications, introduced by Khalifah 'Umar b. al-Khattāb. The Greek-writing officials had been retained in Syria and Egypt and Persian-writing ones in 'Irāq and Persia. By the time 'Abd al-Malik had come to power, the 'Arabs had settled down in the conquered provinces and the local officials had learnt Arabic so much that Arabicization began with full scale already begun by 'Umar and advanced by Mu'āwiyah. With the approval of 'Abd al-Malik in 693 A.D., this change was initiated by the famous school-master and brave general Hajjāj b. Yūsuf in 'Irāq and its eastern dependencies under 'Abd al-Mallk, and Zādān Farrakh and Sāliḥ b. 'Abd al-Raḥmān, a Persian *Mawla* of Sijistan, his experienced secretaries helped Hajjāj in changing the language of the registers. Sarjūn b. al-Manṣūr and his son al-Manṣūr were one after another in-charge of the Syrian *Dīwan* and Sulaymān b. Sa'īd, the *Katib al-Rasa'il* of Walīd completed the translation from Syriac into Arabic. Ibn Yarbū' al-Fazarī translated the Egyptian *Dīwan* into Arabic during the time of Walīd b. 'Abd al-Malik. In spite of the Arabicization of the registers the Persians, Greeks and Copts, however, continued to serve in the *Dīwan* by picking up Arabic. The government officials were not many in number. The tribal chieftains and village headmen were held responsible for maintaining peace and enforcing payment of taxes.

Coinage:—In imitations of the Byzantine and Persian types a few gold and silver coins with Arabic verses had been struck under Hadrat 'Umar and Khalifah Mu'āwiyah under the denomination of *dīnar* and *dirham* respectively. Arabic gold *dīnars* and silver *dirhams* were minted for the first time at Damascus in 76H/695 under 'Abd al-Malik and pure Arabic silver *dirham* was struck at Kūfah in 696 by al-Hajjāj. It bore the legend *Bismillah* and the name of Hajjāj. Under Yazīd b. 'Abd al-Malik, 'Umar b. Hubayrah, the Governor of 'Irāq, minted a standard *dirham* of six *dawaniq*. Hishām raised the standard to seven *dawaniq* but after him the old system of six *dawaniq* was revived. Under the Umayyads the Caliph's name was never struck on the coin even at Damascus and a change of Caliph made no alteration in the coinage. Under the Umayyads weights and measures were also standardised and they were sealed by the Government. A Byzantine weight validated by Walīd I has come to light.

Dīwan al-Khatam:— In order to check forgery *Diwan al-Khatam* (Bureau of registry) a kind of state chancellery was instituted by Mu'āwiyah. It used to make and preserve a copy of each official document before sealing and despatching the original to its destination,[1] previously unsealed orders were being sent out or even delivered to the persons concerned. 'Amr b. al-Zubayr received an unsealed letter from Mu'āwiyah instructing Ziyād b. Abīhī to give the bearer 100,000 *dirhams*. 'Amr opened the letter, altered the figure to 200,000 *dirhams* and received the amount[2] but later it was detected when the Governor sent his accounts. Mu'āwiyah, therefore, introduced this system. The provincial Governor Ziyād also preserved the copies of all his orders[3] and official documents. Thus in the course of time a state archive developed in Damascus by the Umayyads under 'Abd al-Malik.[4] This department survived till the middle of the 'Abbāsid period.

Dīwan al-*Qudat* :—In the early period of Islam justice was administered by the Prophet and the orthodox Caliphs in person. After the expansion of Islamic State 'Umar al-Fārūq had to separate judiciary from the general administration and appointed the first qādī in Egypt as early as 23H/643 A.D. After 661 A.D. a series of judges succeeded one after another in Egypt under the Umayyad Caliphs, Hishām and Walīd II. The judges in the towns

1. Tabari, II, 205-6; Fakhri, p. 149; Ibn Khaldun, *Prolegomenes*, I, 395-6, text/446 tr.
2. Al-Jahshiyari, pp. 24-25
3. Al-Ya'qubi, II, p. 279.
4. Mas'udi, V, 239, see also IV, p. 93 and Ibn al-Athir, VI, p. 49.

of 'Irāq and Arabia were appointed by the Governor of 'Irāq. In the later Umayyad period the governors appointed and dismissed judges as they pleased. They were, however, always appointed from the theologians. These qadis also administered *awqaf* (endowments) and estates of the orphans and the insane.[1]

As the Muslim jurisprudence was not yet codified the Qadis differed in their judgments over similar cases, they sought Caliph's guidance or took signatures of army personnels to enforce their judgment in case the parties did not abide by their decisions. 'Iyād b. 'Ubayd Allāh the Qādī of Egypt sought guidance of 'Umar b. 'Abd al-'Azīz in a case and Sulaym b. 'Anz another qādī of Egypt under Mu'āwiyah took the signatures of army officers over one of his judgments.[2]

'Abd al-Malik had reserved a day for hearing of appeals and complaints[3] and 'Umar II followed him rigidly.[4] This was developed into a full-fledged department, *Nazr fi al-Maẓalim* later under the 'Abbāsids by al-Mahdī.

The non-Muslims enjoyed autonomy as far as the judiciary was concerned, Their own cases were decided by their own judges and Muslim law was not applicable to them in ordinary cases but the cases between a Muslim and non-Muslim were always decided by a Musiim judge or when disputes among non-Muslims took a turn affecting law and order, the Muslim Government interfered.

Shurtah :—Like the early Caliphs the Umayyads had also organised policing of towns and markets. Hajjāj b. Yūsuf (d. 95-714), while governor of 'Irāq under 'Abd al-Malik, appointed 'Abd al-Raḥmān ibn 'Ubayd prefect of police at Kūfah. Adopting harsh measure when he checked the thefts and crimes he was given the police control of Baṣrah in addition to that of Kūfah.[5] The *Saḥib al-Aḥdath* or ***Shurtah*** was not only concerned with the secular side of law but also with the religio-moral side of it during the time of the Umayyads. He was the police as well as

1. Cf. Ibn al-Athir, V. pp. 106, 115, 180 etc.
2. Al-Khudri, II, 355
3. Ibn al-Athir, I, 46
4. Ya'qubi, II, 367.
5. Ibn Qutaybah, *'Uyun al-Akhbar*, p. 33.

municipal head of the city with the headquarters at Damascus the Umayyad capital.

Dīwan al-Barīd:—Ar. *barīd*, perhaps a Semitic word, is derived from Persian *birdan* a swift horse and Ar. birdhawn horse of burden. Some are inclined to derive this term from Latin *veredus* meaning a post horse. Yāqūt the author of the *Mu'jam al-Buldan* writes that the word *barīd* came from the Persian *burīdan* (to cut off) as to distinguish the horse and the postman, the tails of the postal horses were cut off.[2] Many of the terms connected with the *barīd* system are also of Persian origin.[3] The term *barīd* was used by Prophet Muḥammad also.

Mu'āwiyah introduced postal service. 'Abd al-Malik extended it throughout his empire and Walīd made full use of it The Umayyad Caliph 'Abd al-Malik developed a regular postal service.[4] 'Umar bin 'Abdu'l-'Azīz developed it further by building caravanserais at stages along the Khurāsān highway. Relays of horses were used for the conveyance of dispatches between the caliph and his agents and officials posted in the provinces. The main highways were divided into stages of 12 miles each and each stage had horses, donkeys or camels ready to carry the post. Primarily the service met the needs of Government officials and their needs but travellers and their important dispatches were also benefited by the system.. For swift transport of troops also the postal carriages were used. They were able to carry fifty to hundred men at a time. Under its Governor Yūsuf bin 'Umar the postal department of 'Irāq cost 4,000,000 dirhams a year.

The post masters besides performing tbeir usual functions also kept the caliph informed of all important happenings and the officials and chiefs' attitude towards the State and the subject in their respective territories.

Dīwan al-Jund:—The *Dīwan* of 'Umar assigning annuities to all Arabs and to the Muslim soldiers of other races underwent a change in the hands of the Umayyads. The Umayyads meddled with the register and the recipents regarded pensions as the subsistance allowance even without being in active service.

Hishām reformed it and paid only to those who participated in the battle.[1]

On the pattern of the Byzantine system the Umayyads reformed their army organization in general and divided it into five corps: the centre, two wings, vanguards and rearguards while on march or in a battle field following the same formation. Marwān II (744-50) abandoned the old division and introduced *Kurdus* (cohort) a small compact body.

The Umayyad troops were divided into three divisions, infantry, cavalry and artillery. 'Arab troops were dressed and armed in Greek fashion. The Umayyad cavalry used plain and round saddles. The artillery used *'arradah* (the ballista), *manjanīq* (the mangonel) and *dabbabah* or *Kabsh* (the battering ram). The heavy engines, siege machines and baggage were carried on camels behind the army.

Al-Baṣrah and al-Kūfah continued to be the chief military stations. The citizens of both the cities were compelled to provide each a force of 20,000 men by Hajjāj under the threat of withholding the pensions in 80H/699 A.D, and three years after 20,000 men were requisitioned from Kūfah for the campaign in Khurāsān.[2] To supply 2,000 men the Qahtanite chief of Syria was given, 2,000,000 dirhams as annual subsidy[3] and the people of 'Uman were allotted stipends to supply 3,000 men when called upon by Yazīd II.[4] Under the Umayyads Baṣrah and Kūfah were the main recruiting grounds for the army in the eastern zone, while the Syrians and Syrianized Arabs were posted at Damascus. The standing army numbered 60,000 with an annual expenditure of 60,000,000 dirhams including family pensions.[5] The annuities were reduced by 10 per cent under Yazīd III in 744 for which he was called *naqis* (deficient).[6] Under Walīd I the number of annuities in Damascus and its districts reached

1. Wellhausen p. 348
2. Tabari, II, 1944; Ibn al-Athir V, p. 267.
3. Al-Mas'udi, V, 2000.
4. De Goeje, *Frg. Hist. Arab*, I, p. 66
5. Mas'udi, V, 195.
6. Ibn al-Athir, V, 220; Ya'qubi, II, 401

45,000[1] while there were 20,000 pension holders at Hims̩ and its district under Marwān I. Under Marwān II the number of the standing army was increased to 12,000.[2]

The Byzantines were imitated in naval organization. There was a galley of fighting unit with a minimum of twenty five seats on each side of the lower decks each seat having two men. The rowers of the ship who were 100 or more in number were also armed and troops specialized in fighting took up their position on the upper deck. Mu'āwiyah was the father of the 'Arab navy. By the end of his reign there was a fleet of 1,700 ships and in the siege of Constantinople (717 A.D.) an armada of 1,800 ships were employed.[3] At the order of Mu'āwiyah the first Muslim fleet was built at the Byzantine dockyard in Syria. The Umayyads had ship building yards like Seleucia, Tripoli and Tyre on the Syrian coast and Babylon, Aydhāb and Cıysma in Egypt.[4] The most important naval ports of the Abbasid Empire were 'Adan, Sīrāf and 'Umān. Of the second rank were Bas̩rah, Deibul, Hormuz and Kirmān. The Umayyad navy played a prominent part in fighting against the Greeks and occupying the Mediterranean islands. The Umayyad navy was fully organised under Walīd.

Provinces :—For administrative purpose the Umayyad empire was divided into five viceroyalties modifying generally eight provincial units of the preceding Byzantine and Persian empires and later the number of provinces increased as more lands were conquered or as administrative difficulties arose.[5]

1. *Al-'Iraq* comprising most of Persia and eastren Arabia with headquarters at Kūfah which later had a deputy governor for Khurāsān and Transoxiana at Marw and another deputy for Sind-Punjab;
2. *Al-Hijaz* which comprised Yaman and Central Arabia;
3. *Al-Jazīrah* (Mesopotamia) embracing also Armenia, Adharbā'ijan and eastern part of Asia Minor;

1. Cf. H. Lammens, *La Syrie : Precis historique*, Beriut, 1921, I, 119-20
2. Al-Fakhri, p. 197; Abu'l Fida, I, 222
3. Cf. Bury, J. B., *A History of Later Roman Empire*, II, pp. 41-2
4. Al-Baladhuri, p. 144; al-Khudari, II, 212
5. Tabari, II, 1138.

4. *Egypl*; and
5. *Ifriqiyah* (al-Maghrib) comprising North Africa, Spain, Sicily and other adjacent Mediterranean islands with Qayrawān as its headquarters.

The Provincial Secretariat functioned with its various departments under an *Amīr* in charge of the province. The viceroy (*Amīr* or *Walī*) acted as Caliph's representative in the province and was in charge of civil and military administration, tax collection and religious leadership directed by three different officials under him. The Amīr would sometimes appoint his own *'amil* (tax-collector) over a province and would merely seek formal approval of the Caliph. Yazid ibn Muhallab, who was appointed governor of 'Irāq after Hajjāj, appointed his own *'amil.*[1] But very often the revenue was administered by a special officer *Saḥib al-Kharaj* independent of the Viceroy and responsible to the Caliph directly.[2] The *'Āmil's* opinion in the case of revenue was more valued than that of the *Amīr* or *Walī*. Mu'āwiyah had his own *Saḥib al-Kharaj* at Kūfah[3] and two brothers as joint *'amils* of Khurāsān in 58H/678 A,D.[4] Other officials like *Katibs* of the *Dīwan* and *Saḥib al-Ahdath* (police officer) were appointed by the governor himself. Mu'āwiyah's *'amil* in 'Irāq namely Khālid received at the Persian feasts of Nawruz and Mihrjan gift worth 10,000,000 dirhams.[5]

The sources of the revenue remained almost the same as they were under the Orthodox Caliphs. The main sources of the revenue were *Kharaj* (land tax), *jizyah* (poll-tax), *zakat* and *khums* (one-fifth of the spoil). The provincial administrative expenditure was borne by the provincial exchequer and the surplus, if any, was remitted to Damascus.[6] Mu'āwiyah had 2½ per cent deducted as *zakat* from the fiscal annuities of the Muslims[7] like incom tax.

Governors appointed from among the Umayyad princes particularly in the later period had the privilege of ruling over the

1. Tabari, II, 1138
2. Guest, *Kindi* (Gibb Series), pp. 73, 85 , 93
3. Ibn Khaldun, III, p. 4
4. Tabari, II, 188-89
5. Jahshiyari, *Kitab al-Wuzara'*, Leipzig, 1926, p. 11
6. Maqrizi, Khitat, I, 98-99
7. Ya'qubi, II, p. 276

provinces through their Nā'ib (deputies) as most of them were incompetent administrators. Among such princes was Maslamah of Ādharbā'ijān and Armenia who had been appointed by Hishām.

Some of the governors in the provinces acted against the enactments of the centre as they were just, tolerant and benevolent. Against the Covenant of 'Umar, Khālid ibn 'Abd Allāh al-Qasrī, Governor of al-'Irāq under Hishām, built a church at al-Kūfah to please his Christian mother.[1] He granted privileges of building synagogues and churches to the Jews and the Christians and appointed the Zoroastrians to high posts in the government.

Public works :—The Ka'bah which had been rebuilt by Ibn al-Zubayr was restored by 'Abd al-Malik to the form in which it had been left by Prophet Muḥammad.[2] A year later to commemmorate the ascention of the Prophet *Qubbat al-Sakhrah* (Dome of the Rock) was constructed by 'Abd al-Malik at Jerusalem. The Mosque of Madinah was rebuilt with the gold work on the *qiblah* wall which alone cost al-Walid 45,000 mithqals of gold and the Jami' mosque in Damascus cost him 600,000 dinars. Al-Walid also decorated the mausoleum of Prophet Muḥammad. Besides these, old mosques were extended and repaired and many new ones were constructed at the order of Walid. Special care was taken of the wayfarers, the sick and the orphans. Roads were repaired and planted with milestones.[3] Hospitals were established and lepers and persons suffering from infectious diseases were segregated.[4] Blind, incapacitated and limbless persons were granted pensions.[5] Orphanage was opened for the orphans who were given education by the State under the benevolent Caliph al-Walid. 'Umar II had inns built and wells sunk along the roads specially in the newly-conquered countries of the East like Khurāsān and Samarqand. To allow them to reach their destinations, wayfarers were even given money by this caliph.[6] Ponds and tanks were dug on the way to Makkah from Damascus under

1. Ibn Khaldun, I, p. 302
2. Al-Fakhri, p. 177
3. Tabari, I, p. 1191
4. Al-Ya'qubi, 348
5. Al-Suyuti, p. 224; Tabari, II, 1271; Ibn al-Faqih, pp. 106-7
6. Al-Tabari, II, p. 1364

Hishām. Khalid al-Qasri, the governor of Makkah, had a great tank built at the foot of Mount Thabir to supply water to Makkah through lead pipes and got the 'Irāq canal constructed at Wasit.[1] The Governor al-Hur b. Yūsuf built a college and a caravanserai at al-Mawsil during the time of Caliph Hishām. The pensions of the blind and indigent were enhanced and hungry persons were fed from the kitchen of Walid II.[2]

Cities were divided into *al-harras* (quarters) each being independent having houses, mosques, markets, baths and graveyards. Markets and municipal affairs were put under the charge of the town police officer *Sahib al-aḥdath.* Under the Umayyads great importance was attached to the water supply and sewage system of towns. The two sets of channels for supply and clearance of water touched every house of Damascus during the Umayyad Khilafat. They are still in order. The trade guilds occupied separate quarters or streets in the walled city of Damascus situated on the Baradah river, the *Chrysorrhouse*[2] of the Greeks. On the register of Damascus alone there were names of 45,000 pensioners.[3] The two biggest cities of 'Iraq, namely, Baṣrah and Kūfah had good systems of water supply, each house having a *stream.* In Baṣrah alone there were 120,000 streams. During the governorship of Ziyad b. Abihi, the densely populated city of Kufah had in its population, 60,000 strong men to take up arms and their women and children numbered 80,000.[4] To supply al-Mawsil with drinking water Hishām had a canal dug at a cost of 8,000,000 dirhams and a road constructed by the side of the canal was planted with shady trees. Hishām developed agriculture and spent lavishly on building canals and planting gardens. The region of 'Irāq was developed especially through the engineering and drainage works of Hassan al-Nabati. The swamps in the Tigris were dried around Wasit and extensive areas were reclaimed for irrigation and cultivation purposes.

---

1. Baladhuri, ed. de Geoje, pp. 293-4
2. De Goeje, *Fragmenta Historicorum Arabicorum, I, p. 123*
3. De Goeje, *Frag.* I, p. 5
4. Al-Istakhri, p. 80; Ibn Hawqal, p. 159
5. Al-Ma'sudi, IV, p. 194; al-Baladhuri, p. 350

SECTION II

ABBASID ADMINISTRATION

Wazīr :—The Abbasid caliph about whom we have learnt above had an intermediary between himself and his officers and subjects. This officer who introduced envoys and dignitaries into the presence of the Caliph and called *Wazīr* under the 'Abbasids was in charge of an office of Persian origin (*Wazarat*).[1] Caliph al-Saffāḥ instituted the office of *Wazarat* and Khālid b. Barmak was his *Wazīr*. He stood next to the Caliph and acted as *alter ego*. He advised and assisted the Caliph in his administration and as grand *Wazīr* he presided over the council of ministers in charge of various departments. Strong Caliph controlled a *Wazīr* but a weak Caliph was controlled by a strong *Wazīr* who ruled over the empire in his name. As the Caliph indulged in pleasure, the *Wazīr* obtained from him the divine right of kingship. Such right was obtained by Muḥammad ibn Barz al-Qummī through an appointment letter from Caliph al-Naṣir (1180-1225).[2]

The Barmakid *Wazirs* were all-powerful under the Abbasids. They appointed and deposed governors and judges although with the approval of the Caliph. They confiscated the property of the deposed governor as the Caliph appropriated the estates of the deposed *wazīrs*.[3] The sons and brothers even inherited the *Wazīr* as the kinsmen of reigning Caliph did and his sons formed a distinct class, the highest in the official circle. The *Wazīr* wore a black court dress like other Abbasid officials. It consisted of mantle (*darra'ah*), coat (*qamis*), shirt (*mubattanah*) and shoes (*Khuff*). In the 10th century the *Wazīr* was assigned salary of 5,000 and later of 7,000 dinars a month. He even received stipends for his sons at the rate of 500 dinars a month for each.[4] The monthly salary of a *Wazīr* had been a thousand dinars during

1. Ibn al-'Abbas, *Athar al-Uwal fi Tartib a l-Duwab*, Cairo, 1295, p. 62
2. Al-Fakhri, p. 205
3. Ibn al-Athir, V, I, pp. 19-20
4. Khuda Bakhsh, *Renaissanc of Islam*, Patna 1937, p. 89

the time of Caliph al-Mu'tadid bi'llah (892-902).[1] The highest paid minister, the chief of the *Dīwān* al-Sawād (Dīwān al-Kharāj), under Muqtadir (908-932) received 5,000 dinars equivalent to 11,000 dirhams per month. The heads of departments and governors of provinces received usually 300 dirhams a month which they had received under the Umayyads.[2] During the middle period of the Abbasid caliphate the salary of the officials was considerable and included a *qatai'* (fief) also.[3] The Wazīr received valuable presents from governors and other officials. 'Ubayd Allāh b. Yaḥyā ibn Khāqān a very experienced *Wazīr* of Mutawakkil received 200,000 dinars and thirty boxes of Egyptian cloths as present from the Governor of Egypt but he accepted only a handkerchief and deposited the rest in the treasury.[4]

There were two types of *Wazīr* — *Wazīr tafwīd*, minister with unlimited authority and *Wazīr tanfīdh*, minister with limited power to execute only the orders of the Caliph. The minister with limited power did not take any initiative but the *Wazīr tafwid* exercised the powers of sovereignty with certain exceptions. When the Caliph was indolent the *wazīr* gathered unrestricted powers and vice-versa. Some of the *Wazirs* were *de facto* rulers as al-Fadl b. al-Rabi' under al-Amīn and al-Fadl b. Sahb during the early days of Ma'mun's reign. They lost their *de facto* power in the later period of Ma'mūn's reign and under Mu'tasim and al-Wāthiq. The Wazīr Ibn al-Furāt remarked once that his predecessor 'Alī bin 'Isā had administered the government of the kingdom for five years as a *de facto* ruler.[5] The Wazīr could appoint and dismiss any officer except the one appointed directly by the caliphs. In the troubled days of Muqtadir his *Wazīr* appointed officers of the *Diwans*. Ibn Khāqān appointed his own nominees as officials. The *Wazīr* heard all appeals from the lower courts. As a good *Wazir* he exercised general supervision over the State affairs. After al-Wāthiq the Caliph ceased to be the *de facto* ruler and the power passed into the hands of his functionaries led by the *Wazīr*.

1. Hitti, P.K., *History of the Arabs*, p. 319
2. Al-Jahshiyari, *Kitab al-Wuzara*, Leipzig, p. 314
3. cf. Miskawayhi, *Eclipse of the Abbasid caliphate*, ed. & tr. Amedroz and Margoliouth, Oxford, 1920, I, 155.
4. cf. Shah Mu'inal-Din Nadvi, *Ta'rikh-i-Islam*, Part III, *Khilafat-i-Abbasiyah*, Vol. I, p. 240
5. *Eclipse of the Abbasid caliphate*, I, 108

After al-Muqtadir (908-32) the place of *Wazīr* with unlimited power was taken by *Amir al-Umara'* over (Commander of the Commanders) who exercised all the secular power of caliphs although the office of *Khilafat* and *Wazarat* remained but without power.[1] Now the Caliph's *Wazīrs* lost their former position and became known as *Ra'īs al-Ru'asa'*.

The *Wazir* was appointed generally from among the experienced and learned secretaries and scribes of the previous reigns and rarely from the theologians. Towards the end of the third century of Hijri era the *Wazīr* like the Caliph indulged in *ḥaram* life and other activities detrimental to the interests of State so much that he issued blank paper with his signature to be used by his subordinates when required. 'Abbās b. Hasan the *Wazīr* of Muktafī was of this nature. As a result chaos prevailed in the administration from the time of Caliph Muqtadir and annually two or more *Wazīrs* used to succeed one after another. This ultimately led to the appointment of Rā'iq as *Amir al-Umara'* by Caliph al-Rāzī. Even after this though there remained the office of *Wazir* yet he was helpless without power as was the Caliph himself puppet in the hands of *Amīr al-Umara'*.

The *Wazīr* was the head of all administrative departments whose heads were also loosely called as *Wazīrs* often appointed by the chief *wazir* himself. All correspondence passed through the *wazir* who had receiving department called *Dīwan al-Fadd* to open official correspondence and pass on to the ministers of respective departments. The *Wazir* was a president of various central departmental ministries, but every province had at Baghdad its own *Dīwan* (Board) with two sections *Aṣl* (General Administration) and *Zimam* (financial section). Under Caliph al-Mu'tadid (892-902) the Provincial Boards were incorporated into one Central Board under the name of *Diwan al-Dar al-Kabir* with three divisions *Diwan al-Mashriq* (the Eastern Board), *Diwan al-Maghrib* (the Western Board) and *Dīwan al-Sawad* (the Board for Babylon) with one chief dealing with the finances of the three divisions. In the 10th century the general administration of the three divisions were

---

1. Miskawayhi, I, 352.

also amalgamated into one and called *Dīwan al-Usūl* (the Ministry of the Interior) and the Ministry of the Finance was called the *Dīwan al-Azimmah.* As President of the Central Board and Chancellor of the Exchequer the *Wazīr* personally administered the Province of Babylon (*Sawad*). However no sharp line of division was ever drawn between the central and provincial offices.

Diwans :—The number of boards went on increasing and finally the following nine main Boards (*Diwans*) were found functioning at the centre under the Abbasids :—(1) *Dīwan al-Kharaj;* 2. *Dīwan al-Rasa'il* or *Dīwan al-khatam* or *Dīwan al-Tawqi'*; 3. *Dīwan al-Zimam;* 4. *Dīwan al-Nazar fi al-Mazalim;* 5. *Dīwan al-Qudat;* 6. *Diwan al-Shur'ah*; 7. *Dīwan al-Hisbah;* 8. *Diwan al-Barid*; 9. *Dīwan al-Jaysh* (*Jund*).

Dīwan al-Kharaj:—This *Dīwan* dealt with the revenue and its disbursement at the centre having its branches in the provinces. This was the Central Board of Revenue. Of the Departments of State, the Bureau of taxes (*Dīwan al-Kharaj*) was the most important under the Abbasids as it had been under the Umayyads and its chief 'master of taxes' was an outstanding figure among the ministers and was called *Sahib Dīwan al-Kharaj* or simply referred to as *Sahib al-Kharaj.*

Under the Abbasids the revenue departments functioning at the centre were the *Dīwan al-Kharaj*, the *Dīwan al-Diya* and the *Dīwan al-Sadaqah* with two sections of the *Bayt al-Mal*, called the *Khaza'in al-'Āmmah* and the *Khaza'in al-Khassah* and also the *Dīwan Nafaqat al-'Āmmah wa'l Khassah* and the *Dīwan al-Zimam.*[1] Of all these *Dīwan al-Kharaj* was the most important and held some control over other departments and checked the accounts of the *Bayt al-Mal* in the time of Mu'tadid.[2] The *Dīwan al-Zimam* dealt with the auditing of all other departments since the days of al-Mahdi.[3] Aḥmad b. al-Mudabbir headed the *Dīwan al-Kharaj* along with other *Dīwans* until he was transferred to Damascus in 440/854 to be in charge of revenue there.[4] In 245/859 the *Dīwan al-Kharaj* had also a deputy-head in Zaid b. Ibrahīm and a

1. Cf. Ya'qubi, *Buldan*, II, 15; Tabari, III, p. 522
2. Levy, *Social Structure of Islam*, p. 325
3. Ya'qubi, *Buldan*, II, p. 15
4. Ya'qubi, II, p. 596

Mustakhrij (auditor) in Ja'far al-Ma'luf[1] and the *Dīwan al-Diya* had a deputy head in 'Isa b. Farrukhān Shāh. On the advice of Isḥāq b. Ibrāhīm the *Sahib al-Shurtah*, Caliph al-Mutawakkil appointed Yaḥyā the father of 'Ubayd Allāh as head of the department of *Kharaj* and Muṣa b. 'Abd al-Malik as that of *Diya.*[2] The chief treasurer called Mustawfi under the Samanids and the Ghaznawids corresponded to the *Sahib al-Kharaj* at Baghdād and was assisted by *Khazins* (treasurers), *Katibs* (scribes) and *mushrifs* (overseers).[3] The *Dīwan al-Kharaj* also became known as *Dīwan al-Sawad* under Caliph al-M ı'tadid (279-299/892-902). It prepared the revenue demands, receipts and expenditures of the Sawād and distant provinces and maintained general accounts of the Exchequer. It checked all revenue flowing into the *Bayt al-Mal.*

Sources of Revenue:—According to Iṣtakhri and Ibn Hawqal the sources of revenue from the time of Hārūn al-Rashīd to Mu'tadid were the following:-

a) *Kharaj* and *Sadaqah* on land ;

b) the *Jizyah* and *Jawalī* (trade duty) from the *Dhimmi* ;[4]

c) the *Khums* from the mines[5] :

d) the *Mara'i* or pasture tax;

e) *Ghallat* (share-cropping and duty on the mint);

f) the *Marasid* (tolls in the *Diya*[4]);

g) the *Dara'ib* on the shipowners and their merchant vessels[6];

h) *Ajam* (wood);

i) *Athman al-Ma'* (water rates); and

j) *Mustaghilla* (rents on land in the markets of Shiraz and elsewhere and *iqta 'istighlal* from Samarra.[7]

Among the sources of revenue were *Zakat* from Muslims on arable lands, herds, gold and silver, goods etc., *Jizyah* (capitation tax) from non-Muslims at the rates of 4, 2 and 1 *dīnar* per head from capable and earning members, *Kharaj* or '*Ushr* (land revenue), '*Ushūr* (tithes on merchandise), tributes from enemies

1. Tabari, III, p. 1444
2. Ya'qubi, II, pp. 592-3
3. Bayhaqqi, *Ta'rikh-i-Mas'udi*, Calcutta, 1862, pp. 312, 314.
4. Ibn Khurdadbih, 153-4; Ya'qubi, *Buldan*, pp. 2, 10, 123-9
5. *Buldan*, p. 122
6. cf. Istakhri, pp. 156-7; Ibn Hawqal, p. 216; cf. *Kamil*, VII, p. 21 mentions a large impost '*ushr* sale duty on vessels during the time of Caliph Wathiq.
7. cf. Istakhri, p. 156; Ibn Hawqal, p. 217; Ya'qubi, *Buldan*, p. 38.

and truce money. Besides these there were taxes on pasturage, custom duties (*al-Ma'asir*), excise duties and other uncanonical taxes. Cases of forced contributions and fines and confiscation of properties of dismissed or deceased officials were also frequent.

Money collected from Muslims was disbursed for the benefit of the Muslims: the poor, the orphan, the stranger, collectors of *Zakat*, volunteers for the holy war and on ransoming the slaves and captives. The revenue collected from other than *Zakat* was spent on general administration, civil and military.

Kharaj was the most important source of revenue. There existed three types of land-tenure particularly in Fars, Big land holdings, the Measurement system, and the 'Division system; The first was held by landlords who paid lump sum of money to the State treasury, the other two systems were beneficial to the peasanty — the one paid for land brought under cultivation on the basis of measurement of lands and the second paid a share of the crop at the threshing field or its equivalent in cash.

Fiscal Reforms:—Mahdī (775-88) acting on the advice of his Wazīr 'Ubayd Allah increased his income by levying taxes on date palms and other fruit trees. Ma'mūn reduced the taxes from one-half to two-fifths in the Sawād and in 203/818-19 the taxes payable from the city of Rayy was reduced by two million dirhams.[1] Muqtadir (908-32) acting on the advice of h s Wazīr 'Alī ibn 'Isā abolished the *takmilah* system (assessment of *kharaj* in lump sum) in Fārs and made up the deficiencies by levying taxes on fruit trees.[2]

Later Abbasid Caliphs, in order to make up their huge expenditure, resorted to farming out taxes in 'Irāq the system which had been prevalent in Egypt for long. For adjustments with drought and other natural calamities contracts (*iltizam* or *qabalah*) were made to the tax-farmers (*multazims*) for four years and allowances were made for building or repairing dykes and digging channels at the rates mentioned in the schedule. As a consequence the old *qata'i* lands particularly in Egypt were transformed into military fiefs yielding increased revenues.[3]

---

1. Al-Fakhri, p. 260
2. *Wuzara,* pp. 140-41
3. *Kitabu'l Wuzara'*, Leipzig, 1926, pp. 10-11; Maqrizi, *Khitat,* I, p. 83.

In the first century of the 'Abbasid khilafat the revenue was on the increase, but from the following century it was steadily on the decline. Details of the annual revenue received from the provinces during the reign of Hārūn (786-809) based on the treasury receipts for a year are given by Jahshiyārī.[1] During the time of Ma'mūn besides taxes in kind 27,800,000 dirhams were received annually in cash from al-Sawād (Lower 'Irāq), 28,000,000 from Khurāsān, 23,040,000 from Egypt and 14,724,000 from Syria including Palestine and 331, 929,000 dirhams in total excluding taxes in kind from all the provinces.[2] A few years later possibly under Mu'tasim (833-42) the taxes both in kind and cash came 130,2000,000 dirhams from al-Sawād, 37,500,000 from Egypt, 15,860,000 from Syria-Palestine and 381,291,350 from the whole of the empire.[3]

Historians and geographers are silent as regards the expenditure but casually they refer to the amount available in the treasury at the death of a caliph which clearly indicates the surplus left after covering the expenditure of the State including public works and royal expenditure and speaks of the flourishing condition of the country under such rulers. On the death of Manṣūr there were found 14,000,000 dīnārs and 6,000,000,000 dirhams in the treasury at Baghdād[4] while Hārūn al-Rshīd died leaving 900,000,000 dīnārs[5] and Muktafī (d. 908) left behind 100,000,000 dinars in the treasury.[6]

Crown Lands.—Besides the public '*ushri* and *kharaj* lands there were crown (*khas*) lands and personal estates of the caliphs and princes. For their administration and maintenance there were departments called *Dīwan al-Sawafī* and *Dīwan al-Diya* respectively. Al-Manṣūr appointed his mawla, Sa'īd, to be in charge of his *Diya'* (estates).[7] The *Dīwan al-Diya'* and the *Dīwan al-Sawafī*

1. Cf. *Wuzara*, pp. 82-3; Levy, *Sociology of Islam*, I, 343
2. Ibn Khaldun, *Muqaddamah*, pp. 150-51 : Cf. Huart, *History des Arabs*, I, p. 376.
3. Qudamah, *Kharaj*, pp. 117-51 : Huart, I, 176 : cf. also Ibn Khurdadbih, p. 5 seq for the revenue in the first half of the third century of Hijra era but his total does not tally with the details given by him : cf. Zaydan, *Tamaddun*, II, p. 61
4. Mas'udi, VI, p.
5. Tabari, III, p. 764
6. Tha'alibi, *Lata'if*, p. 71
7. Al-Jahshiyari, p. 119

of Hārūn's time corresponded to the two branches '*Ammah* and *khassah* of the *Dīwan al-Diya'* under al-Mutawakkil.[1]

To meet the contingent expenses of the palace and the court, to deal with the salaries and the provision of their men and to take care of the stables there was a board called *Dīwan al-Nafaqat*. All these three boards were concerned with the personal properties of the caliphs and princes and requirements of the courts, palaces and stables.

Revenue Calendar :—From the early days of Islām the practice was to calculate revenue in terms of the lunar year. In respect of the payment of *Jawalī* and *Sadaqah* lunar year was followed in the towns and solar year in the villages.[2] The *jizyah*, *sadaqah* and taxes on hereditary tenements and mills were calculated by the lunar month and taxes on harvests according to the convenience of the cultivators (solar year)[3] Along with the lunar calendar (354 days a year), the local solar calendar was followed e.g. Coptic year of 360 days, the Persian year of 365 days and the Greek year of 365¼ days. Although the assessment of taxes was made on the basis of lunar year, the bulk of the revenue was collected on the basis of the local calendar (solar year).[4] Harvesting began about the time of the *Nauruz* (the Persian New year's day) which generally fell on 17 Hajiran but by 242/856 in 243 years the *Nauruz* had advanced by two months and *kharaji* year had receded by 60 days and the Hijri era had advanced by 7 years at the rate of one year in every 33 years. Realizing the difficulties of the peasants Mutawakkil revised the fiscal calendar, solar and lunar, to the convenience of the taxpayers by intercalating the lunar year in terms of the solar year and by registering the revenue of 241/855 and 242/856 under one year and issuing order in Safar 242/June-July 856 to this effect.[5] Balādhurī, a courtier of Mutawakkil, expressed his doubt in the accuracy of the conversion of the corresponding dates made by Ibrāhīm b. 'Abbās al-Suli in his draft of the circular order.[6]

1. Al-Jahshiyari, p. 177, Ya'qubi, II, p. 516.
2. Ibn Hawqal, pp. 308, 341 ; *Khitat*, II, 19-22, 39-41, 44 ; cf. Mez, *Renaissance*, pp. 107-8
3. Muhammad Shamsuddin Miah, *The Reign of al-Mutawakkil*, pp. 148-49
4. *Khitat*, II, pp. 19-20, 39-41, 44
5. *Khitat*, II, 41-44
6. *Irshad*, II, pp. 128-9 quoted in the *Reign of al-Mutawakkil*, p. 152

Al-Mutawakkil's reforms were discontinued by his successors till it was revived by Mu'tadid in 282/895. According to al-Bīrūni[2] while al-Mutawakkil began the calculation from the beginning of the reign of Yazdgird III, Mu'tadid chose the date of the fall of the Persian Emperor. Al-Bīrūni further observed that both were wrong and their calculation was short by 17 days representing the earlier neglect of the Persians themselves e.g., intercalation of 60 days instead of 77 days.

Dīwan al-Rasalat :—To handle all official letters, mandates, diplomas and other state papers there was a board of correspondence or chancery office called *Dīwan al-Rasalat.* In the Central secretariat the *Dīwans* of *al-Rasa'il* (*al-Risalat*) and *al-Khatam* (*al-Tawqi'*) were very significant under the Umayyad and Abbasid Caliphs. The *Sahib Dīwan al-Rasa'il* drew up the imperial mandates, diplomas, political correspondence and took royal decision on petitions in the public audience. His *dīwan* had a section of secrecy (*al-Sirr*).[3] The *Amīd al-mulk*, the King's confidential secretary, was the head of the *Dīwan al-Risalat* or Chancery under the Samanids and Ghaznawids[4] by which orders were issued and despatches were made to the province and accounts of royal household was maintained. An official of the Chancery accompanied the army to send daily despatches to the King. Under the Fatimids this department was called *Diwan al-Insha'*.[5]

The *Diwan al-khatam* worked till the reign of the Abbasid Caliph al-Amin (d. 814 A.D.). It lost its importance when the power of the Caliph was usurped by the *wazirs*, *amirs* or *sultans.* Meanwhile *Dīwan al-Tawqi'* was introduced by Harun al-Rashid or even earlier than him substituting *Dīwan al-Khatam* ultimately. *Dīwan al-Tawqi'* was also known as *Dīwan al-Rasa'il* as they were so much corelated and interconnected that it was difficult to distinguish one from the other.

The Caliph's decision (*tawqi'*) was written by his secretary on petitions and other documents. Sometimes the Caliph himself

---

2. Chronology, p. 37 quoted by Shamsuddin Miah.
3. Al-Jahshiyari, p. 117
4. Cf. Bayhaqqi, *Ta'rikh-i-Mas'udi,* Calcutta, 1861, p. 161; Jahshiyari, p. 181
5. Cf. *Wuzra,* 183; Maqrizi, *Khitat,* I, p. 274; Qalqashandi, *Subh al-A'sha,* 93-110-111.

wrote his *tawqi'* on the petition under his signature. If such orders were applicable in other cases also they were copied and circulated to governors and officers concerned as it was done once when Caliph Mu'tadid passed an order on a petition for the postponment of a date for the payment of *kharaj.*[1] Before circulation such orders were entered into a register. Because of its privileged position as the office could exert political power this *Dīwan* was called *Dīwan al-Tawqi' wa'l Tatabbu' al-'Ummal* (the office of Decision and of Supervision over Officials).[2]

Dīwan al-Azimmah :—To control the departmental account and to audit the accounts of the *Dīwans* a separate department under the name *Dīwan al-Azimmah* (the Chief Auditing Department) was introduced by Caliph Mahdī. There was maintained in this *Dīwan* a register (*Zimam*) of each department. To supervise all dealings concerning revenues and lands there was *Dīwan al-Zimam al-kharaj.*[3] The Head of this State Chancery (*Dīwan al-Azimah*) audited the accounts of provincial governors (*Dīwan al-Zimam* in the provinces).

Dīwan al-Nazar fi'l Mazalim :—To listen grievances against injustice done and to set matters right in administrative and political departments there was *Dīwan al-Nazar fi al-Mazalim*, a board for the inspection of grievances e. g., the supereme court of appeal. Umayyad caliphs being less accessible to the public had to set apart sometimes for hearing appeals and inspection of grievances. The office of *Dīwan' al-Nazar fi al-Mazalim* was thus introduced by 'Abd al-Malik but developed into a full flaged department for criminal appeal under the Abbasids. Al-Mahdi and his successors al-Hadi, Hārūn and Ma'mūn received complaints in public audience.

The Caliph himself acted as the Supreme court of Appeal. He heard complaints in public audience and redressed the grievances of the people. Hārūn appointed Ja'far to preside over the Board. Ja'far once decided more than thousand cases in a single day and

1. Cf. Jahshiyari, *Wuzara,* Leipzig, 1926, 183 ; Maqrizi, *Khitat,* I, 274 ; Qalqashandi, *Subh al-a'sha,* I, 93
2. Tabari, III, 1440
3. Tabari, III, 522; *Khitat*, I, 274 ; Jahshiyari, *Kitab al-Wuzara,* p. 183.

all were found correct on verification.[1] u nday was set apart for deciding cases of *al-mazalim* by al-Ma'mūn on whose order the *qadī* heard a case between a woman and the Caliph's own son.[2] This institution of *nazar fi al-mazalim* functioned efficiently up to the time of al-Muhtadi (869-70) and was introduced into Sicily by the Norman King Roger II (1130-54).[3]

Dīwan al-Shurtah (the Police Department) :—This was an institution of Police established by Hadrat Alī. It was headed by *Sahib al-Ahdath* under the Umayyads and *Sahib al-Shurtah* or *Wali al-ahdath wa'l ma'awin* (prefect of the police) under the Abbasids. He was the chief of police as well as of the royal bodyguard under the early Abbasid Caliphs and executed death sentences.[4] During the decadent period of the Abbasids his importance grew so much that he occasionally held the rank of a *wazīr* besides presiding over a *dīwan*.[5] He was a well-paid officer but his jurisdiction was confined to cities. Each important city had its own special police whose function was semi-police and semi-military in character.

The title of *Sahib al-Shurtah* (Commander of the Bodyguard) was first given to the governor of a province or a town who settled all matters of dispute. Under the Abbasids it was reserved for a special official responsible for order and public security and he had greater power than the *Qadī* held. He was empowered to take action on mere suspicion and to threaten any one with punishment even before proof was established. Suspected persons were put into prison in order to make investigations or tortured in order to force confession.[6] Under the Abbasids only citizens of the lower classes, particularly all suspicious individuals and persons of evil repute, were under his power although in Spain *Shurtah al-Kubra* (Grand Police) could take legal proceedings even against high officials if they had been guilty of crime.[7]

Dīwan al-Hisbah :—Under the Abbasids a separate department was instituted by Mahdi to look after the municipal and market

1. Jahshiyari, p. 240
2. Al-Mawardi, Chapter VII
3. Amari, M., *Storia dei Musulmani di Sicilia*, III, Catalonia, 1937-9, p. 452
4. Ibn al-Athir, VI, pp. 16-17
5. Ibn Khaldun, *Muqaddamah*, I, 452
6. Abu Yusuf, *Kitab al-Kharaj*, p. 107
7. *Encyclopaedia of Islam*, IV, p. 393 ; Imamudin, *Socio-Economic and Cultural History of Muslim Spain, Leiden*, 1965, p. 52.

affairs, to prevent commercial knavery and to establish religious principles and public morals. The chief of this department was called *muhtasib* who acted as overseer of markets and morals. He was to see that proper weights and measures were used in the market. He dealt with the cases of fraudulent sales and non-payment of debts. To maintain approved morals in the city he checked gambling, usury and sale of wine. In performing his functions he was a police officer-cum-magistrate. Although he stood between a *qadī* and a police chief, in rank and power he was inferior to both of them.[1] In some respects his duties were parallel to those of a *qadī* but as soon as evidence was sifted and oaths were administered, his jurisdiction ceased. He was, however, empowered to whip drunkards and culprits on the spot. He was also to see that people kept the fast and performed their prayers in the mosque and, if a mosque fell into disrepair, he called the attention of the authorities to the matter. He prevented cruelty to servants and animals, enforced *'iddah* (the period of waiting after divorce or death of husband) and encouraged marriage. References are also found in histories to the effect that in the office of *hisbah* deaths and births were registered and orphans' property was administered.

Dīwan al-Qudat :—Like other Muslim rulers the Abbasids also considered the administration of justice as a sacred duty and entrusted it to an independent class of officials called *Qadis*. To dispense justice al-Mahdī the Abbasid Caliph established a separate institution of justice under the name of *Dīwan al-qudat* and appointed Abū Yūsuf, an illustrious pupil of Imām Abū Hanīfah, Chief Judge (*Qadī al-Qudat*) at Baghdād. Henceforth the Chief Judge appointed *qadīs* (judges) in the provincial and district towns from among the *fuqaha* (theologians). Abū Yūsuf (d. 798) served as *Qadī al-Qudat* under al-Mahdī and his two sons al-Hādī and Hārūn.[1]

The early Abbasid Caliphs including Mansūr appointed their own judges like the Pious Caliphs and early Umayyad Caliphs[2]. In 772 the *qadi* of Egypt was appointed by Mansūr and then

1. Ibn Khallikan, II, 334
2. Ya'qubi, *Historiae*, ed. Houtsma, II, Leyden, 1883, II, 468

again the *qadi* of Madīnah was later appointed by al-Mahdī. At a later stage, however, the *wazirs*[1] and governors appointed and dismissed judges. As a prince of justice the *Qadī* often did not rise to receive a governor and sometimes not even a *Wazīr* while on the contrary the wazīr Ibn 'Abbād had to offer his hand to help the qādī in getting up [2] Under Ma'mun, a Qādī of Egypt refused to allow a *barīd* to have seat with him in the court and another Qādī of Egypt, namely Ibn Harbawayhī (third century A.H.) refused to call on and pay his respects to the governor of Egypt namely Ibn Bistām.[3] The judges used to be Muslim, male, adult, mentally and physically sound and well-versed in the Islamic laws[4] having the power of independent judgment (*ijtihad*). The judicial seat was reserved for the Qādī as he was the representative of the commander of the Faithful.[5]

The judges were of two types with special and limited authority (*Khaṣṣah*) and absolute and general authority (*'ammah mutlaqah*).[6] The power of the second class judges was limited and restricted by the appointment letters issued by the Caliph, *Wazīr* or Governor. Besides deciding cases, the Qādī of the first class acted as guardian for orphans, lunatics and minors, administered pious foundations (*awqaf*) and the estates of orphans, imbeciles and other persons and drew up contracts of marriage for women without male relations. He imposed punishments on those who violated laws. He also led the Friday congregational prayers and appointed his deputies (*na'ib*) in the provinces and districts. In the early period of the 'Abbasids before Mahdī the provincial judges were appointed by the governors but in the fourth century Hijrah they were appointed by the *Qadī al-Qudat* of Baghdād. The judges were paid handsomely. Under al-Ma'mūn, the judge of Egypt received 4,000 dirhams a month.[7] The Qādī was one of the high officials in the city and commanded respect from the

1. Ibn al-Furat, *Nishwar al-Muhadara*, p. 115
2. Cf. Yaqut, *Irshad*, II, 339; cf. Suyuti, *Husn al-Muhadara*, II, p. 101.
3. Quoted in the *Renaissance of Islam*, p. 217.
4. Al-Mawardi, pp. 107-11
5. Al-Kindi, ed, R. Guest, Leyden, 1912, pp. 444, 524
6. Ibn al-Furat, pp. 117-25
7. Suyuti, *Husn*, II, p. 100

citizens. The Abbasid Qādī wore the black official dress and from the 9th century he used *danniyah* (a high conical cap).

Diwan al-Barīd:—The postal bureau (*barīd*) was introduced by the Umayyads and developed further under the Abbasids. Mail service was another Persian institution like *al-Khatam* introduced by Mu'āwiyah to carry official mails and despatch news regarding happenings in remote provinces to the Caliph and to keep the officials in check. It was organised and improved by 'Abd al-Malik using relays of horses and camels between Damascus and the Provincial towns. It was re-organised on a new basis by Hārūn through his Barmakī tutor-counsellor Yaḥyā b. Khālid. The head of this institution called *Sahib al-Barid* supervised the officers of the post-roads and was incharge of their salaries. He had intimate knowledge of the itineraries and advised the Caliph on his tours and despatch of his troops. Besides handling primarliy the State correspondence the postal institution served the public interestes although in a limited way on payment of a substantial sum.[1]

There was a post office (*barīd*) in each provincial capital and roads were constructed by the Abbasids connecting Baghdād with leading commercial centres of the empire.[2] Relays of horses and mules or camels were posted along these routes covering vast distances to carry message, to transport soldiers with their baggages and to carry newly appointed Governors to their respective provinces.[4] The Abbasid Caliph once sent a *shal* to Ibn Tūlūn in Egypt through *Barīd*.[3] For relays camels were used in Arabia and Syria and horses and mules in Persia. Relays of donkeys and camels had been posted by the Abbasid Caliph Mahdī between the main towns of Makkah, Madīnah, Baghdād and others.

The news service of the Abbasid Empire had been highly developed. To carry secret news and to transmit news quickly the services of homing pigeons were utilised. As letter carriers the pigeons were trained. The news of the capture of the rebel Bābak, Chief of the Khurrami sect, which arose as a result of the

1. Mas'udi, VI, p. 93
2. Ibn Khurdadbih
3. Ibn al-Athir, IV, pp. 373-4
4. *Ibid.*, VI, p. 49

execution of Abū Muslim Khurāsānī, was transmitted to al-Mu'tasim by pigeons in 837 A.D.[1] Signalling by fire was also of great importance used generally at the time of enemy's movements.

Postal directories indicating itineraries of the whole empire with various stations and the intervening distances were prepared for the guidance of postal messengers. The directories were also used by travellers, pilgrims and soldiers and were utilised as a source for writing works on geography. One of the earliest Muslim geographers worked as *Sahib al-barīd* in al-Jibal (ancient Media) during the time of al-Mu'tamid. He was Ibn Khurdādbih (d.ca 912) who wrote *al-Masalik Wa'l-Mamalik* (Road Book) utilising the materials available in the archives and postal directories.

Caravanserais, hospices and cisterns were constructed along the main roads. Along the Khurāsān road Caliph 'Umar b. 'Abd al-'Azīz had built such *Khans*(inns).[2] By the building of *khans*, the digging of wells and the establishment of security forces along the roads, private traffic also received impetus under the Abbasids.

The postal department served as a bureau of intelligence and the Postmaster-General was the chief of an espionage system and was therefore called *Sahib al-barīd wa'l Akhbar*, Controller of the post and intelligence services.[3] He was, therefore, an inspector general of espionage and a confidential agent of the khalīfah.[4] Thus he used to gather information about the activities of provincial governors, other officials and chiefs from provincial postmasters whose spies (*'ain*) supplied him with such informations. The postmaster even informed the Caliph directly. In 822 Mā'mūn was reported by the *Sahib al-Barīd* of Khurāsān that Tāhir the governor of the province had omitted the Caliph's name from *khutbah*. Al-Mutawakkil while he was out of capital once received report through *barīd* against the governor of Baghdād about his indulgence in *haram* pleasure and negligence of duty. The Abbasids had a well established system of espionage

1. Mas'udi, VIII, pp. 126-7 ; Joseph Hell, *The Arab Civilization*, tr. by S. Khuda Bakhsh, Lahore, 1943, p. 79.
2. Ibn al-Athir, V, p. 44
3. Qudamah, p. 184
4. Atlidi, *I'lam al-Nas*, Cairo, 1297, p, 161 quoted by Hitti, *History of the Arabs*, p. 995n3

even beyond the own empire in the Byzantine territory. Merchants, pedlars and travellers acted as detectives for al-Manṣūr and Hārūn al-Rashīd, while 1,700 aged women were employed in the intelligence department by al-Ma'mūn. The *Diwan al-Barīd* was thus the head quarters of the intelligence service of the State.

The duties assigned to a postmaster were mentioned in his appointment letter. As mentioned in the appointment letter of a Postmaster dated 314/927, among his duties were the reporting in detail on tax-collectors, cultivation, the condition of the people, living-standard of judicial officers, minting of coins and the supervision of the office dealing with government pensions.[1] Besides supplying secret news, matters of interest were also reported by the postmaster as was done once in 300/912 by the postmaster of Dinawar.[2] Extracts of important reports were made and kept in the file of the head office.

Under Caliph Manṣur the *Sahib al-Barīd* of each district submitted daily report on (*a*) the price of food-stuffs, (*b*) the cases decided by a qādī, (*c*) the workings of executive and revenue officers, (*d*) the revenue returns of the treasury and (*e*) other important matters. Inspite of the protests made by Nizam al-Mulk, the Saljuq Sultan Alp Arslān (1069-72), however, discontinued the *barīd* in the Eastern Caliphate.

Dīwan al-Jund (*Jaysh*) :—*The Dīwan al-Jund* was resposible for the recruitment of the solidiers and the payment of their salaries It was introduced by 'Umar I, by the early Umayyads, reformed and rectified by Hisham and continued under the Abbasids. All soldiers irrespective of their nationalities on participating in a war were granted stipends and allowances.

The Army :— Mu'āwiyah created a disciplined army from the raw Syrian soldiers on whose loyalty he depended chiefly and replaced the tribal organization by a well-planned military machinery after the Greek pattern. While the early Abbasids drew their soldiery from the Khurāsānis, later, they depended on the supply

1. *The Renaissance of Islam*, 78.
2. *Ibid.*, 79

of new recruits from among the Turks and Berbers and re-organised the army on the Persian pattern under Persian and Turkish generals.

The Abbasid army was composed of regulars and irregulars Among the regulars besides *al-haras* (bodyguards) there were *junds* who were permanently on active service and were called *murtaziqah* (regular force) and, at the time of need, the irregulars who were recruited from the Bedouins, peasants and townsmen, were called *mutatawwt'ah* (auxiliary force).[1] The irregulars were more in number and received rations only while on duty and share in the *ghanīmah* (war booty). The standing army was never big under the Abbasids. The caliph's bodyguards formed the nucleus of the army. They were better equipped with arms and uniforms and they received a higher salary than others. Under Mā'mūn, when the Abbasid Empire reached its zenith, there were 1,95,000 soldiers in the army and infanty men received 240 dirhams and the cavalry men double of this a year[2] while from the first Abbasid Caliph to al-Amīn, besides receiving rations and allowances, a foot soldier received on the average 960 dirhams a year.[3] The soldiers were well-paid and comparatively better-off when their emoluments are compared with the daily wages of masons and labourers engaged in the construction of the city of Baghdād under al-Manṣūr, the master builder receiving a dirham and the ordinary labourer about a third of dirham a day.[4] Under Ma'mūn the salary of a clerk of central secratariat was 120 dirhams a year.

The *Dīwan al-Jaysh* (the war office) had a recruiting department (*Majlis al-Muqabah*) and a department of pay (*Majlis al-Taqrīr*). There was a section called *Dīwan al-Ard* for the inspection of military equipments.[5] The army was composed of the infantry (*harbiyah*), cavalry (*fursan*) and archers (*ramiyah*). The footsoldiers were armed with spears, swords and shields and the horsemen used helmets and breast-plates for their defence and long lances and battle-axes for offence. The Persian way of wearing swords round the waist was preferred to the old

1. Tabari, III, pp. 1008 seq. ; Ibn Khaldun, III, 260
2. *Ibid.*, III, pp. 830, 867
3. *Ibid.*, III, p. 41 ; Ibn Athir, V, 322
4. *Ibid.*, III, 326 ; Ibn al-Knatib, I, 70
5. Al-Jahshiyari, p. 365.

'Arab system of carrying it over the shoulder under al-Mutawakkil.[1] The naptha-throwers (*naffatun*, the Greek fire) wearing fire-proof suits and hurling incendiary material at the enemy were attached to the archers.[2] To besiege a fort or a city the army was accompanied by an engineering unit with catapults, mangonels and battering-rams. An engineer, Ibn Sābir al-Manjanīqi, wrote a book on the art of warfare in details during the reign of Abbasid Caliph al-Nāṣir (1180, 1225)[3]. Credit goes to Hārūn al-Rashīd for the introduction of field hospitals and ambulances of litters carried by eamels which also accompanied the army on the battlefield.[4]

Under the Abbasids the army personnel of the Persians began to increase and those of the Arabs diminish. The Arabs, Persians, Turks, Berbers, Negroes and others were recruited as soldiers without any racial or colour bar under the Khurāsānī troops gradually to be replaced by the Turks later. As usual, the 'Arab soldiery was divided into two divisions the Mudarites and the Yamanites and neo-Muslims were attached to some 'Arab tribes belonging to either of the two divisions. Adding one more of the Khurāsānis, there were formed national divisions by al-Mansūr the virtual founder of the Abbasid dynasty. Two more divisions one consisting of the Turks and the other of the Africans were added to the army by al-Mu'tasim. Turkish slaves from Farghanah and other parts of Central Asia and Berbers from Africa were recruited in the army. With the introduction of Turkish slave-troopers the Khurāsānī elements were relegated to the background.

Peace was threatened within the capital because of the large scale employment of the Turks in the bodyguard. It crushed resenment among the people of Baghdād leading to the construction of the city of Samarra on the eastern bank of the Tigris in 836 to accommodate the Caliph and his bodyguard. The Turkish influence continued to increase so much that about twenty five years afterwards, on the death of al-Muntasir (861-2), the Turkish body-

1. Ibn Khaldun, III, 275; Khuda Bakhsh, *Orient under the Caliphs*, p. 340, 344-45
2. Aghani, XVII, 45 ; Ibn Khaldun, III, 260
3. Ibn Khallikan, III. 397
4. In Spain Hajib al-Mansur's dead body was brought on camel's back.

guards became the determing factor in state affairs. During the period of one century of the Buwayhid rule the Turks and the Dylamites of the Caspian Sea region were equally strong and often rioted until at last the Saljuqs came and the supremacy of the Turks was re-established finally.

The officer of every ten men of the army was an *'arif*, of every fifty, a *khalifah*, of every hundred, a *qa'id* and of ten battalions each consisting of 1,000, an *amīr* (general). A company was constituted of 100 soldiers and several companies formed a *Kurdus* (cohort). The Abbasid army was strong enough to suppress revolts in Persia, Syria and Central Asia and to fight against the Byzantines. After the introduction of the foreign units by al-Mutawakkil the army lost both morale and discipline and the decline of the Abbasid military power began.

During the decline of the Abbasid Caliphate there started the practice of granting fiefs (*Iqta'*) to members of the armed forces in lieu of pay. Al-Muqtadir (908-32) farmed out provinces to governors and military commanders sowing the seeds of a feudal military system in the empire. The *Iqta'* (farming) system was further developed under the Buwayhids and it was made systematic under the Saljuqs. The military generals received towns and regions over which they ruled, paid an annual tribute to the Buwayhid or Saljuq *sultans* and supplied troops only on demand.

The Navy ;—Mu'āwiyah was the first Muslim Caliph to take initiative in the development of navy. By the end of his reign there was a fleet of 1, 700 ships in the siege of Constantinople in 48H/717 an armeda of 1,800 vessels were employed[2] although the navy had to withdraw on account of the Greek fire thrown by the garrison on the advancing Muslim fleet and land force. Although the Umayyads, ship-building yards at Seleucia, Tripoli and Tyre on the Syrian coast and Babylon and Clysma on the Nile in Egypt were further developed under the Abbasids yet special attention was paid to the naval development in the Persian and Arabian water. The fleet was divided into five squadrons with headquarters at Seleucia (Latakia in Syria), Tunis (Ifriqiyah), Alexandria (Egypt), Babylon (the Nile) and a special squadron at Farāmah at the

1. Tabari, III, 1799 ; Mas'udi, VI, 452 ; Ibn Khaldun, III, 299
2. Burry, J.B., *A History of the Late Roman Empire*, II, pp. 41 seq.

mouth of the Nile. From the protected and fortified military harbour of Tyre operations were directed against the Greeks in the Eastern Mediterranean waters.

The sphere of Muslim navigation was divided into two separate zones, the Indian Ocean and the Mediterranean Sea, with two separate shipping systems while the ships were stiched in the first one, they were nailed in the second one. The Muslim merchant navy became important as early as under the Umayyads. Under the Abbasids, the Muslim merchants traversed the Indian and Pacific Oceans. Seleucia became the most important centre of trade in Syria under the early Abbasids. It was fortifited by al-Mu'tasim. The merchandise coming from the Mediterranean region passed through the Nile to Aswan or Qus from where it was carried by land to 'Aydhāb, the Red Sea port. Among the sea ports, Aden on the Red Sea coast and Sīrāf on the Persian Gulf, were the most important, the less important ones being Baṣrah (the Sawād or the *Shat al-'Arab*), Hurmuz (Kirmān) and Deibul (Sind). Under the early Abbasids from levies of the shipping at Sīrāf alone there was an annual income of 2,53,000 dīnārs.[1] There was overwhelming Arab influence on the nautical life of the Europeans.[2]

Provinces :—The provinces formed more or less a loose confederation within the Caliphate. The Umayyad division of the empire into provinces was increased and their sizes were reduced. The number of provinces had reached thirty-six although the number and size of such provinces varied from time to time.

To bring greater order in the system of administration, the simple administrative machinery of the Umayyad period was elaborated under the Abbasids. Under the Umayyads Arabia and Khurāsān sometimes formed single province, at other times they were split up into several provincial units if the governor happened to be weak. Under the Abbasids the big and unruly provinces were divided into a number of sub-provinces. Thus there were twenty-four major and twelve minor provinces (fiscal units) under Hārūn and Ma'mūn. The major units like Khurāsān and Egypt had a complete set of provincial officers and *Dīwans*. Physical units

1. *Journal of Royal Asiatic Society*, 1912, p. 188
2. Imamuddin, *Some Aspects of the Socio-Economic And Cultural History of Muslim Spain* (711-1492), Leiden, 1965, pp. 190-200.

remaining almost the same, the political divisions varied from time to time and became big or small according to the status of the governors.

Like Walīd b. 'Abd al-Malik, Hārūn al-Rashīd had also divided his empire into *al-Maghrib* and *al-Mashriq* with Ja'far al-Barmakī and his brother al-Fadl al-Barmakī as their viceroys respectively.[1] During the time of Ma'mūn, al-Fadl bin Sahl was the Viceroy of the East and called *Dhu al-Riyastayn* (the master of two domains, e.g. war and states).

Because of distance and geographical features, the governors of far-flung provinces tended to become supreme in all local affairs and their office hereditary. The governors were appointed by the caliph but on the recommendation of his *Wazīr*. Like the *Wazīr* the Governor (*Amīr*) was of two types one with unlimited power called *'Imarah 'Ammah* (general amirate) and another with limited power and restricted authority called *'imarah Khaṣṣah* (special amirate). The former had jurisdiction over judges (*qadis*) and tax-collectors (*'Amils*) but the latter not. But this was all in theory. In practice a strong governor exercised his authority in excess of what he was given during the time of the weak caliphs and decentralization started with its unavoidable consequences.

The *Amīr* (commander of the army) and the *'Āmil* (tax-collector) stood side by side at the head of the provinces. The two heads of the province, although sharing the same ceremonial privileges at court functions and receiving their general order from the *Wazīr* simultaneously, yet the *Amīr* was higher in rank as he had the privilege of leading the Muslims to prayer. The *Amīr* and *'Āmil* of Fars and Kirmān joined together in 319/931 and stopped remittance of revenues to Baghdād for long.[1] When the two posts of *Amīr* and *'Āmil* were held by one man he was the lord of the province. In 325/937 the Turkish general Begkem accepted the offer only when he was appointed *Amīr* and *'Āmil* of Khuzistan.[2] Officially the position of Aḥmad ibn Tūlūn and of Ikhshid was that of an *Amīr* although they ruled over Egypt independently. The Ikhshids gave fixed salaries to officers and the Fatimids followed their policy.

1. Zaydan, *Tamaddun*, II, pp. 37,44 ; Le Strange, *Eastern Caliphate*, I, 184.
2. cf. Al-Jahshiyari, p. 230.

Governorship had become hereditary even under the Umayyads, and more so under the Abbasids, resulting in the split up of the Abbasid Empire into small principalities accepting generally the nominal suzerainty of the caliphs. Three such principalities in al-Maghrib and one in al-Yaman were established in the early days of the Abbasids. Idris, a brother of al-Nafs al-Zakiyab, escaped to Tangier from the battle-field of Fakh and laid the foundation of the Idrisid dynasty there with the newly constructed city of Fez as its capital. Aghlab was a successful viceroy of Ifriqiyah, an unruly province, which received 100,000 dinars from the revenue of Egypt to balance her deficit budget. His son Ibrāhīm obtained an autonomous status from Hārūn al-Rashid on the promise of remitting 40,000 dīnars annually to Baghdad in stead of receiving a subsidy to cover the expenditure of the province. Yaman also, for all practical purposes, became independent under Muḥammad ibn Ibrāhīm, a descendant of Ziyad bin Abihi, who established his headquarters at Zabid in 204AH/-819-20 and ruled over al-Yaman and Tihamat al-Yaman. He and his successors were the Abbasid governors only in name otherwise they ruled independently. Gradually several other independent principalities also arose in the East.

Local expenditure was incurred from the local income and if any surplus left, it was sent to the central exchequer by the governor and, in case of deficit, he used to receive money in order to meet the expenditure from the central treasury which was concerned with the expenditure of the court, the ministries and Baghdad or Samarra.

All the important central *Dīwans* had their branches in the provinces and to minimise the expenditure sometimes two or more central *dīwans* had only one in the provinces. Thus after amalgamation there were eight main *dīwans* in the provinces and they were *Dīwan al-kharaj*, *Dīwan al-Rasa'il*, *Dīwan al-Zimam*, *Dīwan al-Barīd*, *Diwan al-Jaysh*, *Dīwan al-Shurtah*, *Dīwan al-Qudat*, and *Dīwan al-Hiṣbah.* Among the local officers, as for example in the small town of Raqqah on the Euphrates, there was com-

1. Ibn-al-Athir, VIII, p. 165
2. *Ibid.*, p. 252.

mander of the garrison who also held the office of *Saḥib Ma'unah* (Chief of the Police), a *qadi*, a tax-collector, a post-master and an administrator of the crown lands (*Sawafi*). Considerable portion of revenue was spent on irrigation and public works.

For the development of agriculture specially in Egypt and 'Irāq special attention was paid by the provincial government at the instance of the Centre. Thus the silte4 old canals were re-dug and new ones were excavated forming a veritable network.[2] Among such canals mention may be made of *Nahr 'Isa* connecting Euphrates with the Tigris in the north-west at al-Anbār and Baghdād respectively, Sarāh being its chief channel. *Nahr Sarsar* connected the Euphrates with the Tigris above al-Madā'in, and Nahr al-Malik entered the Tigris below al-Madā'in. Still below there were *Nahr Kuthah*, the *Nahr Dujayl* (diminutive of Dijlah) and the Great Sarāḥ with an innumerable irrigation channels.[5] Al-Mahdī dug the *Nahr al-Silah* in Wāsit with a bridge across it having five doors for the passage of boats one big and four small ones of eight yards each.[7] The 'Abbasid Caliph Hārun entertained the idea of digging a canal through the Isthmus of Suez with a view to facilitate trade between the Red Sea and the Mediterranean Sea.

With the elaborate irrigational works, many swampy regions were reclaimed, silted canals were re-excavated and all-round economic development witnessed the 'Abbasid period. With the economic changes corresponding changes were brought in social structure under the 'Abbāsids. The 'Arab aristocracy was relegated to the background and the Persian Mawālis took full advantage of the situation. Thus a new aristocracy mostly of the Persians grew. They amassed wealth by holding lucrative jobs and by having additional facilities through land-holding, banking and trade.

Public works:— After establishing themselves firmly the Abbasids were prone to devoting their energy and time to development works; for the convenience of the pilgrims, rest-houses were

1. Ibn Hawqal p. 166.
2. *Ibid.*, 165-6; Cf. Istakhri, pp. 84-5
3. Yaqut, III, 377-8
4. *Ibid.*, II, 555; Istakhri, pp. 77-8
5. Baladhuri, 291/451

constructed at reasonable intervals from Qadisiyah to Makkah and milestones were planted along the road by al-Saffāḥ. Tanks were constructed at every stage and the court of K'abah was further enlarged by al-Mahdī. The Caliph changed the *ghilaf* of the K'abah annually, removed the *Maqṣūrah* and reduced the height of the *Minbar* (pulpit) to that of Masjid Nabawī.[1] The cathedral mosque was built in the city of Baghdād by Manṣūr and the suburbs had many parks, gardens, *ḥammams* and markets. Because of the great development in agriculture and industry, living became cheap and people became happy under Manṣur. Fat was sold at six seers a dirham, honey at five seers a dirham, olive oil eight seers a dirham and mutton three seers a dirham.[2]

The city of Baghdad was extended towards the east on the left bank of the *Tigris* under the name of al-Mahdiyah by Caliph al-Mahdī. There were 10,000 public baths (*ḥammams*) which were used by women also on specific days. There were 27,000 baths in the city under Muqtadir (295-320/907-931) and later their number rose to 60,000.[3] About 300/212-13 there were 27,000 mosques in Baghdād which had a population of 2,000,000.[4] The city of Baghdād was divided into two portions, east and west. To look after the western portion of Baghdād there was a governor and the eastern portion was under the direct control of the court.

In 161/778 al-Mahdi built up military stations on the road from Baghdād to Makkah, set up milestones and dug wells to supply water to the pilgrims. Two broad roads were constructed across both the sides of the Euphrates. As regards the communication of the city, a net work of high roads was constructed none of which was less than forty cubits broad. Al-Mahdī, like his great predecessor Walīd b. 'Abdu'l Malik, took great care of the sick and the poor. Lepers were provided with pensions. Mahdī patronised the '*Ulama*', released the prisoners and returned the confiscated properties of the people.[5] The Caliph's agent called *Amīn* kept him informed about the conduct of the officials, their

1. Ya'qubi, II, 475; Mas'udi, II, 229-34
2. *Ta'rikh al-Khatib*, I, p. 70
3. Al-Ya'qubi, pp. 250, 254; *al-Khatib*, pp. 117-118
4. Al-Khudari, Vol. III, p. 134
5. *Ta'rikh al-Khulafa'*, p. 276

justice and moderation. To provide the sick with food and medicine hospitals and dispensaries were established under the care of the Barmakids who hailed from the high priestly family of the Buddhist monastery of Nawbahar in Balkh.[1] Medical education was also imparted in these hospitals and astronomy was taught in the observatory attached to *Bayt al-Hikmah.* The observatory of the Shammāsiyah gate of Baghdād became known as *Rasad Ma'mūn.*[2] Under Mā'mūn's special care Baghdād rose to prominence socially and economically. The markets and shops were full of native products and foreign goods were imported from China, the Malayan Archipelago, India, Scandinavia, Russia and East Africa. Translators like Nasturi, Ya'qubī, Sābī, Majusī, Rumī and Brahma all from 'Irāq, Syria and Persia gathered in Baghdād which became a rendezvous of art and science.[3]

Hārun died leaving behind 900 million dīnārs in the treasury which speaks of the prosperity of the Empire and development of the economic resources of the lands. In 830 Mā'mūn established at Baghdād the famous *Bayt al-Hikmah* which was a combination of library, academy and translation bureau.[4] The chief of the translators, Hunayn b. Isḥāq, was appointed superintendent of *Bayt al-Hikmah.* Al-Khawārizmī (d. 850) based his astronomical tables (*Zijj*) on al-Fazārī's work. In 771 A.D. Muḥammad b. Ibrāhīm al-Fazārī had translated the Indian work *Sidhanta* (*Sindhind*) on astronomy into Arabic at the instance of al-Manṣur.[5] The *Nestorian* Jurjis or Jaur Jais (George) b. Bakhtyishu', the dean of the hospital of Jundishāpur, was invited and appointed a court physician by al-Manṣur in 765. His son Bakhtyishu' worked as the Chief physician of the Baghdād hospital under Hārun al-Rashīd. The family members of Jurjis served as court physicians of the Abbasids for about 250 years. Hārūn invited Mankah, an Indian physician, to Baghdād and got the Indian medical books translated into Arabic. *Al-Hawi* of Abū Bakr Muḥammad al-Rāzī (Rhazes, 865-925) and *al-Qanūn* (*Canon*) of Abū 'Alī Husain

1. *Cf.* Syed Sulayman Nadvi, *Arab Hind Ke Ta'alluqat*, pp. 102-3
2. *Cf. Tabaqatu'l Umam*, p. 50
3. Jurji Zaydan, *Tamaddun-i-Islam*, III, 142
4. *Cf.* Mulla Kalib Chalibi, *Kashf al-Zunun*, p. 447; *Tabaqatu'l Umam*, pp. 52-55; *Akhbaru'l Hikmah*, pp. 22-23
5. *Tabaqatu'l Atibba*, I, 123-4

ibn Sīnā (Avicenna, 980-1037) became supreme in medical science in Europe for centuries.

Like the water channels in 'Irāq there were road-net-works spread throughout the Abbasid empire, the main being Bag͟hdād to Cyrenaica, Bag͟hdād to Syria, Bag͟hdād to Chinese Turkistān, Marw to Farg͟hanah, Naysābur to S͟hīrāz, Bag͟hdād to Makkah, the Romman highway extended by the Muslims from Damascus to San'a' in Yaman and the other one from Fustāt to the Atlantic ocean along the Mediterranean coast. These roads were used by travellers and merchants and for military movement and postal despatch. Books were written on them by the Abbasid geographers like Ibn K͟hurdādbih and Iṣtak͟hrī under the titles *al-Masalik wa'l Mamalik*.

Manṣur elaborated the postal organisation and made the postal directors record every day happenings in their jurisdiction, officers' conduct and even the nature and quantities of corn sown in the fields and despatched to him daily. Mahdī posted relays of donkeys and camels between the main towns of Makkah, Yamāmah and Bag͟hdād. To cross the major rivers, ferries were employed but on less wide rivers and canals bridges were built on arches of stones and bricks. There were also bridges of boats. For the protection of the travellers, policemen were posted along the roads and inns were provided with food, fodder and water.[1]

Elaborate arrangements were made by the Abbasids also to supply water to metropolis (*al-misr*), city (*al-qaṣbah*) and town (*al-Madīnah*). Bag͟hdād abounded in fresh water canals which sprang mostly from the Tigris.[2] There were also reservoirs and two covered aqueducts built of bricks and lime.[3] To supply water to Makkah which suffered from the scarcity of water during Hajj time underground aqueduct at a cost of 1,500,000 dinars was constructed by Zubaydah, grand-daughter of Manṣur and wife of Harun al-Ras͟hīd. The defect in the aqueduct which obstructed water occasionally was rectified under the instructions of Mutawa-

1. Al-Istakhri, p. 290; Al-Maqdisi, p. 418
2. Ibn al-Khatib, Vol. I, p. 111-117
3. Al-Ya'qubi, *Kitab al-Buldan*, p. 250

kkil's mother.[1] The systems of water supply in Samarqand,[2] Naysābur,[3] Carthage[4] and Qumm[5] were also praiseworthy.

Mills were erected in Baṣrah, as elsewhere, at the mouth of the canal fed by the tide and driven by the receding water at the time of ebb.[6] There were floating flour mills on the Tigris in Baghdād and elsewhere. The floating flour mills of Mawṣil were made of wood and iron and were suspended on iron chains in the mid stream, each having two stones (*arbah*) able to grind fifty camels' load a day.[7] In Baghdād the largest mill, the Patricious Mill, had 100 stones and earned annually 100,000,000 dirhams a fabulous sum.[8] In the 4th/10th century there were wind-mills in Afghanistan for grinding wheat. These mills were run by a strong and steady wind especially during two months in the winter and two months in the summer. These were made exclusively for it having eight arms and standing between two posts which allowed wind to penetrate like a wedge. The arms were placed vertically standing on a similarly perpendiculer rod, "the lower end of which sets in motion a mill stone which revolves over another stone."[9] They had hatches (*manafis*) which were opened or closed to have more or less wind.[10]

Of the hydraulic machines used in 'Irāq and elsewhere by the Muslims were *Na'urah*, *Dulab* and *Daliyah*. *Na'urah* was introduced by the Persians to pump water from a low level to a higher one and were driven by animals or the current of a river. This Persian wheel consists of a rope, five heavy wooden buckets. two small and a large wheels with teeth, a long pole of thirty palms etc.[11] *Dulab* which was the Persian name for the Greek *manganon* and the Roman *cigognet* was used in between Baghdād and Anbār and was run by oxen and camels.[12] *Al-Dāliya* a synonym of

1. Tabari, III, p. 1440
2. Al-Istakhri, p. 216; Ibn Hawqal, p. 866
3. Al-Maqdisi, p. 394
4. Yaqut, IV, p. 58; Mez, *Renaissance of Islam*, p. 413
5. Al-Ya'qubi, *Buldan*, p. 274
6. Maqdisi, p. 125
7. Al-Bakri, p. 162
8. Ya'qubi, p. 243 quoted by Khuda Bakhsh in the *Renaissance*, p. 467
9. *Ibid.*, p. 467
0. *Ibid.*, p. 467
1. Imamuddin, S. M. *The Economic History of Spain*, Dacca, 1965, p. 77
2. *Cf.* Ibn al- Jawzi, *Manaqib Baghdad*; Le Strange, p. 67

Na'urah was very much common as an instrument of irrigation.[1] *Al-Daliyah* and *al-Rahba* which lay on the western bank of the Euphrates belonged to Malik ibn Tauq of the Banu Taghlib tribe in the reign of Ma'mun. Besides *Na'urah*, *Dulab* and *Daliyah* other hydraulic machines like *Zurnuq* and *Manjanun* were used for irrigation purpose in other parts.[2]

Riverine communication in 'Iraq and Egypt was better and sometimes even quicker than by land. The Tigris and Euphrates were the best means of communication between Baghdād and the district towns. Through them the towns were also joined with the Persian Gulf having Baṣrah at the mouth of the Tigris as a port for sea-going boats. The Tigris being navigable even in its upper part was better than the Euphrates from the navigational point of view.[3] At the beginning of the 4th/10th century the number of boats in the port of Baghdād had reached 30,000 and the daily import of corn was worth 9,000 dirhams.[4] Some canals were also used for nevigational purpose up to Nahrawān. In 215/917 'Alī bin 'Isā, an efficient wazir of al-Muqtadir (908-32), sent 300 boats *via* the international trade route of Nahr 'Isā and Nahr Sarāt from the Tigris to the Euphrates.[5] The barges sailed to al-Muhawwal one farsakh from Baghdād in the west to unload into small boats which sailed to Baghdād through Nahr 'Isā.

There were police posts (*Mahtat*) along the water routes to guard the merchants and travellers.[6] The booths (*al-Hawanit*) lay on the eastern bank of the Tigris.[7] In the beginning of the 10th century to collect tolls, barriers were moored at Dayr al-'Aqul (the convent of the loop river) across the Tigris by *Aṣhab al-Sayyara wa'l Maasir* (Masters of Travellers and Barriers). Two boats were moored on the one bank of the Tigris, opposite to two other boats on the other bank and these two likewise were firmly moored. Cables were carried across the stream being fastened

1. JRAS, 1895, p. 70
2. Baladhuri, p. 180; Yaqut, II, pp. 534, 764; JARS, 1895, pp. 67, 70; Le Strange, p. 105
3. *Mafatih al-'Ulum*, p. 71 quoted by Khuda Bakhsh in *The Renaissance*, p. 450
4. Al-Tanukhi, II, 205; Al-Suli, *Akhbar al-Radi wa al-Muttaqi bi'llah*, p. 122-3
5. *Cf.* Al-Maqdisi, p. 124; Ibn al-Faqih, p. 270
6. *Cf.* Ibn Khurdadbih, p. 154; *Kitab al-Buldan*, p. 324
7. Ibn Rustah, p. 185

to boats on either side of the river. Boats were then prevented from passing at night without paying tolls. There were also stations for officials, travellers, merchants and customs.[1]

To administer a town properly there were five main officers an *'Āmil*, a *Qadī*, a *Saḥib al-Shurtah*, a *Saḥib al-Hisbah* (*Muḥtasib*) and a *Sahib al-Barīd*.[2] Many of the cities were governed by a council of notable citizens (*Diwan al-Shūra*) whose members were nominated by the government. There were merchant guild with Amins as their members and *Ra'īs al-Tujjar* as their presidents to supervise commercial transactions. The towns where most of the functions of the government were performed by the citizens themselves were self-sufficient and semi-independent units like the free cities of Europe. To look after the cleanliness, sanitation and comforts of the citizens, there was a supervisor in each quarter or block of the towns. There were proper arrangements for lighting the streets, markets and parks in Baghdād and for the removal of night soil. To maintain discipline in public places and to look after the purchase and sale of goods in the markets and municipal affairs there were *Muḥtasibs* in Baghdād and other big cities.

The municipal administration and public works as introduced by Umayyad and Abbasid rulers may occupy a prominent place in the history of administrative development of the world. Even today their municipal activities claim admiration of modern statesmen and engineers.

The municipal administration usually referred to the public services rendered by the state to a city and a village to confer on the citizens the amenities and privileges of various kinds.

There were five categor es of towns in the Muslim world :

(*i*) Hellenistic Mediterranean type;

(*ii*) South Arabian type, in which the streets were very narrow and houses several storeyed high;

(*iii*) Mesopotamian and eastern type;

1. Ibn Rustah, pp. 184-5; Le Strange, p. 36; JARS, p. 46
2. Ibn Hawqal, p. 309

(*iv*) **Iranian type in which the town consisted of three distinct parts, fortified area for the army, official quarter and commercial quarter, each separated from the other by a wall; and**

(*v*) **Garden town, as towns of Madīnat al-Zahrā near Cordova and Sāmarrā ih 'Irāq. In later constructed towns the houses stood aloof and were decorated with trees and plants.**[1]

1. This is a revised and enlarged edition of the chapter on Administration in *A Political History of the Muslims*. Vol. II (Umayyads and Abbasids)

CHAPTER IV

UMAYYAD ADMINISTRATION IN SPAIN[1]

The Umayyad Empire was divided into two viceroyalties, the Eastern and the Western. The more important one was that of al-Maghrib (West) with its headquarter at Qayrawān. It was divided into seven districts Barqah, Ifriqiyah, Tahirat, Sijilmāsah, the Mediterranean islands of Sicily, Sardinia and the Balearic islands, Spain and Southern France. Spain was ruled by a governor called *Amīr* or *Walī*. The capital was shifted from the Gothic headquarter of Toledo to Seville and finally to Cordova. The civil and military administration of the country was in the hands of the Governor but the collection of revenues was the task of the 'Āmil, who was wholly independent of the *Amīr* and directly appointed by the Khalīfah. The Governor was appointed by Khalīfah and sometimes by the Viceroy of Ifriqiyah if he was strong and the Khalīfah was weak. He ruled almost independently, although nominally he was subject to the Viceroy of Ifriqiyah. The tenure of his office was subject to the caprices of his two masters. He laboured under a two-fold disadvantage, being subordinate both to the Viceroy and the Khalīfah. This division of loyalty was not conducive to good government. It encouraged the leading party of the Arabs to depose one *Amīr* and set up another and the approval of this change had to come in due course of the time from the Khalīfah or Viceroy. The provincial officer like *Sahib al-Kharaj*, *Qadī*, the *Ka'ibs* and others were appointed by the *Amir* or *Khalifah.*

The Amīr or khalīfah :—An end to his dual subservience was put by 'Abd al-Raḥmān I in 756 A. D. by breaking Spain away from the Khilāfat of Baghdād. The earlier Umayyad rulers continued to call themselves as Amīrs till 929 A. D., the year the Umayyad Amir 'Abd al-Raḥmān III assumed the title of Khalifah caused the *khutbah* to be read and coins struck in his name. He

1. A revised edition of the chapter on Administration in ***A Political History of Muslim Spain,*** **Dacca 1967, pp. 333-351.**

was the supreme temporal and spiritual head of the State. Although he held a hereditary office he was sometimes raised to the throne by the nobles. Living in pomp and grandeur he appointed a *ḥajib* to carry on the civil administration, a *qa'id* and a *qadī* to discharge military and judicial duties respectively. A strong Amīr or Khalīfah was always the arbiter of all governmental affairs and did not tolerate any intrusion on his right nor on the rights of any of his subjects. He not only appointed officers to look after the well-being of the subjects but also reviewed his troops and toured the provinces. When at leisure he spent his time in the company of poets, philosophers and scientists for the advancement of learning.

Offices :—The Central government offices were housed in Alcazar at the Bāb al-Sudda near the Cordova bridge. The machinery of government under the Caliph was broadly divided into three departments, *viz.*, finance, judiciary and military which were independent of one another. The high posts in all these departments were held generally by the 'Arabs and Berbers and the lower ones were filled by the neo-Muslims, Christians and Jews. The headquarters of all these institutions were located around the Umayyad palace at Cordova. Although no special training was required for holding a post of distinction, experience was very much counted. Highly educated and experienced officials knew something of everything and were, therefore, transferred from one department to another or held two or more distinct posts at a time.[1] The civil executive officers, therefore, acted sometimes as military and judicial officers as well.

Wazarat :—While the Independent *Amīr* or *khalifah* was the supreme head of government, the actual administration of the country was run by his *wazīrs* (ministers). Instead of *wazīrs*, 'Abd al-Raḥmān I had a number of *Shaykhs* to assist him with their experience and advice.[2] Each *wazīr* was in charge of a particular department. There were four principal departments, *viz.*, Finance, Justice, Foreign Affairs and War. The promotion

1. *Cf.* Ibn 'Idhari, *al-Bayan*, II, pp. 205, 211, 213; Levi-Provencal, *L' Espagne*, p. 62.
2. Gayangos, II, p. 91.

of any one to the post of a *wazīr* did not necessarily mean the abandonment of his previous office. By promotion he was included in the nobility and entitled to receive a higher salary.[1] Sometimes a minister was in charge of two offices, known as *Dhu'l Wazaratayn.* Ibn Shuhayd held two such posts in the Umayyad period and Ibn al-Khaṭīb had the same privilege in the Naṣrid period. In Spain he was neither a representative (*na'ib*) of a Caliph nor was he a chief minister as the word *wazīr* denoted in the 'Abbasid East. He approached the Khalīfah through the prime minister, known as *ḥajib* in Umayyad Spain.[2]

The *ḥajib* being next to the Caliph screened the Khalīfah from the eyes of his subjects as the word indicates. As president of the Council of Ministers,[3] he represented the Caliph in all state affairs, dealt with all the royal mandates, administered the country and led military expeditions. A member of the royal family or a man of very exalted position, well-versed in civil and military administration, was usually offered this dignified post.[4] During the regime of the weak rulers the *ḥajib* practically ran the entire show of administration.[5] He appointed and deposed ministers, governors and judges, though in theory he sought the approval of the *khalīfah.* Gradually he became the king-maker and his office became so important that some petty rulers took pride in calling themselves as *ḥajibs* in the eleventh century

Khuttah (Secretariat) :—The *Khuttah* was another equally important administrative machinery. Its function was to look into all State affairs and to control all income and expenditure. It was headed by a Chief Secretary in charge of *khidmat al-khilafah.* He was almost equal in rank to a *wazīr* and received the same salary. The secretariat was divided into two departments under the charge of *Katib* (*Sahib*) *al-Rasa'il* and *Katib al-Dhamam* (*Ṣaḥib al-Ashghal al-Kharajiyah*). The first dealt with the royal correspondence and the other with public finance.

The Katib al-Rasa'il as head of the department of correspondence took parts in the deliberations of the Council. By the

1. Ibn 'Idhari, *al-Bayan*, II, p. 195.
2. *Cf.* Gayangos, II, p. 150: *Levy*, *Sociology of Islam*, II, 26
3. *Cf* Levi-Provencal, *L 'Espagne*, pp. 64, 66; Ibn al-Abbar, *Hullah*, p. 137.
4. *Cf. L 'Espagne*, p. 64
5. *Cf.* Gayangos, II, p. 92

middle of the 10th century the department of correspondence gradually grew into so much importance that it was divided into some sub-offices About this time Jahwar ibn Abī 'Abdah worked as chief inspector of all correspondence relating to the central government.[1]

The *Sahib al-Rasa'il* corresponded with *Sahib al-Barīd* (the office-in-charge of postal organization). Besides his usual function the *Saḥib al-Barīd* supplied the King with the information of activities of the officials and subversive movements of officials and chiefs. Along the roads post-offices were set up. Although the postal service was for the government, it accepted urgent private letters and other official objects like presents. Pigeon post was used for speedy delivery and to signal serious danger, beacons were lit on the tops of hills.

Sahib al-Ashghal, the head of the department of Public Finance, was empowered to impose taxes, to receive revenues and to make disbursements. In practice he was more powerful and influential than a *wazīr* and kept the province in awe by means of his overseers and tax-collectors. His duties were performed by a *wakīl* under the Naṣrids of Granada.

Justice :—The *Amīr* or *Khalīfah* was the highest judge and heard special cases. Normal judicial administration was carried on by a judiciary consisting of the Chief *Qadī* at Cordova, *qadīs* in cities and *ḥakims* in small towns. The Chief *Qadī* was called *qadī al-qudat, wazīr al-qadī* or *Qadī al-Jund* (judge of the brigade) who was posted at the military district (*Kurah*) headquarters to administer justice among the Syrian 'Arab tribes who had settled there at the beginning of the 8th century.[2] The *qadī al-Jund* used to be chosen from among the neo-Muslims and he became known as *qadī al-jama'* (judge of the congregation). The Chief *Qadī* ranked among the dignitaries of the State and had his seat with the *wazīrs* at official ceremonies. For his guidance he had a council of jurists called *majlis al-shūra* or *aṣḥab al-ra'ī*[3] to give counsel at crucial moments in disputed matters. He held so much power

1. Ibn 'Idhari, II, p. 236
2. Al-Maqqari, II, 92
3. Levi-Provencal, *L' Espagne*, p. 81

that he could summon even the ruler to his presence. Ibn Bashrī (d. 823 A. D.) the Chief *Qadī* did not hesitate to pass judgement against the *Amir* and made him pay compensation to a suitor and on another occasion he refused to accept the testimony signed by the *Amir* who had to appear in the court to give his evidence before the Chief Qādi.[1]

In the 10th century the post of Chief *Imam* of the Mosque and Chief *Qadī* often used to be held by two different persons. The Qādī was in charge of *Bayt al-Mal al-Muslimin*, preserved in the *maqsūrah* of the Cordova Mosque[2] and administered *awqaf* (endowments) and the properties of the orphans and insane. The *Qadīs* posted in the provincial and district headquarters were the deputies of the Chief *Qadī* and performed all his duties. The Chief Judge of the military courts was *Qadī al-'Asakir*.

In the judicial hierarchy of Cordova next to the Chief *Qadī* ranked the *Sahib al-Mazaiim*, *Sahīb al-Radd*, *Sahib al-Shurtah*, *Sahib al-Sūq* or *Muhtasib* and *Sahib al-Mawarith* (official in charge of inheritance.)

Cordova had another special judge called *Saḥib al-Maẓalim*. He was appointed by the *Amīr* to hear cases of breach of privilege, discipline or of offences committed by public officials. *Saḥib al-Radd* was to hear cases of complaint against the judges. *Saḥib al-Radd* and *Saḥib al-Maẓalim* were often one and the same officer.[3]

The non-Muslims had their own judges to administer justice according to their own laws. But cases between a Muslim and a non-Muslim were decided by a Muslim judge.

The usual punishments inflicted were fines, scourging, mutilation and, in cases of heresy and apostasy, death.

Subordinate to the *Qadī* was a city magistrate called *Saḥib al-Shurtah*, whom the common people called *Saḥib al-Layl* and *Saḥib al-Madīnah* (the Night-guard and Chief of the city); but by the 10th century the two officials became independent of each other. Sometimes the *Qadī* and *Saḥib al-Shurtah* were one and the same man. The office of the *Saḥib al-Shurtah* was located near the Palace gate. His duties consisted of detecting and

1. Al-Maqqari, pp. 109-112
2. Cf. Ibn 'Idhari, *al-Bayan*. III, 98
3. Levi-Provencal, *L' Espagne*, p. 95

punishing crimes against the public morals or the civil regulations of the city or district entrusted to his care. The head of the police was under the direct control of the Governor. The Chief of the police in the provincial towns known as *Sahib al-Ahdath* stood half-way between the police and the regular soldiery. His duty was to prevent disturbances and other crimes.

The municipal police was under the command of a especial officer called *Muhtasib,* who belonged to the class of the *Qadis*. In the beginning the market officer was called *Saḥib al-Sūq* or *Wali al-Sūq* but by the end of the 10th century he became known as *Muḥtasib* and *Wullat aḥkam al-ḥisbah.*[1] The *muḥtasib* was the superintendent of the markets as well as the public censor. While inspecting the markets and examining weights and measures, he publicly flogged cheats and swindlers. He also dealt with all cases of gambling, sexual immorality and indecency in dress. In special cases he was empowered to inflict very severe punishment like cutting off of hands and even executing death sentences.[2]

A town inhabited by the people of different races, religions and tribes was divided into several quarters. It was walled around for defence purposes and each quarter was separated by walls with gates. There were night watchmen called *al-Darabūn* to close the city and quarters' gates after evening prayer preventing any communication during the night and at the times of disturbances. The *Darabūns* were well-armed and had watch-dogs and dark lanterns. There were watch towers called *atalayahs* at strategic points to watch the frontier towns. Coastguards were posted to keep watch against pirates. Patrols and sentinels were posted on the roads at regular intervals for the safety of travellers and merchants.

Provincial Government :—For administrative purposes the whole country was first divided into five main provinces :

1. Andalusia, the country in the south situated between the Mediterranean Se. and the Guadiana river;
2. Central Spain, the country between the Mediterranean and Lusitania in the west and the Douro river in the north;
3. Galicia and Lusitania (modern Portugal);

---

1. *Cf.* Ibn Bashkuwal, I, p. 152 : Ibn al-Faradi, I, 46.
2. *Cf.* Ribera, *Aljoxani*, pp. 178-9/220-2 tr.

4. The country on both sides of the Ebro; and
5. Septimania, southern France.

But as the country developed and the administration centralized, the size of the provinces was reduced for better administration and each important town with its surrounding lands became a province. In the 10th century, these provinces corresponded to the military districts (*kuwar* pl. of *Kurah*) and the three marches (*thughūr* pl. of *thaghr*), e.g., Lower, Upper and Middle Marches. The two vital points of the frontier in the caliphate period were the towns of Saragossa and Toledo.

Each of these provinces was placed under a civil and military governor called *walī*. The district officer was called *ḥakim*. The *Khalīfah's* duties devolved on the governor. One of his main duties was to render military assistance to the *Amīr* or *Khalīfah* at Cordova. During the dependent *'Imarat* period when the area covered by the province was large he had two or more lieutenant-governors posted in important cities and a military commander on the frontier. The *walī* had about six ministers to administer the affairs of minor importance in their respective districts. He toured the country to settle the disputes of the people and replaced the *qa'ids* and city magistrates guilty of dereliction of duty. The governor was, in general, a *qa'id* (military general) and belonged to a local aristocratic family of the Arabs, Berbers and of neo-Muslims. He sometimes paid a fixed portion of the revenue of the province to the ruler of Cordova.[1]

The governor posted in the frontier provinces was a military chief of great importance and held more power than the governors of other provinces. He belonged generally to the family of the Ṭujibids, Banū Hūd, Banū Razīn or Banū Dhū al-Nūn. During the period of decay of the Umayyads it was the frontier governor who declared his independence first.

Revenue :—Among the principal sources were land-tax, *zakat*, *jizyah*, customs and market duties, mine tax and booty. During the time of 'Abd al-Raḥmān III, the main sources of revenue as described by Ibn Hawqal were *jibayah* (land-tax), *kharaj* (tributes

1. Ibn 'Idhari, *al-Bayan*, II, p. 153

from Christian vassals), *zakat*, minting of coins and import, export and market duties.[1] For the collection of these taxes an office after the name of *Khuttat al-Ashghal* was created at Cordova. The head of the revenue department was *Khazin*, also known as *Sahib al-Makhzan*, a man generally of aristocratic family.[2] Hakam I entrusted the task of collecting taxes in his Kingdom to the Christian Rabi, son of Teodulfo.[3] The Jewish physician and politician Hasdai ebn Shaprut held an important post perhaps in the customs department.[4] In the 11th century a contemporary writer Ibn Hazm complains against the Jews' rough and harsh method of collecting illegal taxes called *mukūs*.[5]

The lowest branch of the finance department was located in the villages and supervised by divisional head called *'Āmil.* The harvest being ready, the field was inspected and the value of the produce was estimated by an officer called *'ashshar*.[6] There was a mutaqabbil to collect market and other duties within the fiscal area of his *qabalah.* In order to check these officers from cheating and charging more than the dues, strict vigilance was kept on them.[7]

An account register was maintained and census was taken during the time of Yūsuf al-Fihrī and the bishop Hostegesis prepared a complete descriptive list of tax and *jizyah*-payers during the time of Muḥammad I and made annual visits to see that the taxes were properly realised.[8]

The rate of land-tax generally varied from 1/6th to 1/3rd according to the quality of the land. The practice of collecting the tax on cattle in kind was given up by the Umayyad *'Amirs* but that of land-tax in kind or cash continued. The land-tax collected in kind during the time of Hakam I amounted to 4,700 *mudd* of wheat and 7,747 *mudd* of barley.[9] 'Alī b. Hammūd (1009-1018 A.D.) ordered the people of Jaen to pay the land-tax in cash at the rate of six dīnārs for a *mudd* of wheat and three

1. Kramers, *Ibn Hawqal*, 108
2. Levi-Provencal, *Histoire*, III, p. 30
3. *Ibid*., I, p. 162, III, p. 32
4. *Ibid*., II, p. 69, III, 32
5. *Al-Andaulus*, II, 1934, p. 35/88 tr.
6. Levi-Provencal, *Histoire*, III, p. 39
7. *Cf*. Gomez, Emilio Garcia, *El Tratado de Ibn 'Abdun*, pp. 104-8
8. *Cf*. Lopez, *Contribuciones*, pp. 96, 104
9. Gayangos, I, p. 213

dīnārs for that of barley instead of paying in kind.[1] Muslims paid *zakat* at the rate of 2½% on their wealth and young earning members of non-Muslim families paid poll-tax (*jizyah*) varying from 12 to 48 dirhams (£ 1.5 to £ 5) a year in monthly instalments. from, There were custom-houses in big and small towns, commercial centres and ports. Idrīsī speaks of an office of *Rihadrah* (the custom-house) at Lorca and Himyarī of that at Qalab.[2] Arms, war-horses, books and bridal ornaments were exempt from import duties.[3] Goods for personal consumption were also exempt from such duties.[4] After meeting the expenditure of local administration, the amount of taxes deposited in the local treasury was passed on to the provincial *Bayt al-Mal* and from there the balance was transmitted to the Central headquarter at Cordova[5] which controlled all the treasuries of the country and replenished the coffer of a province which fell short of fund.[6] The taxes collected from the *mustakhlaṣ* (the royal land) were passed on directly to *Bayt al-Mal al-khaṣ* (the royal treasury) for the personal expenses of the ruler. The royal *Khas* lands accumulated in the provinces due to the confiscation of lands from the nobles from time to time. The administrative head of the royal property was *Saḥib al-Diya'*.[7] The annual revenue from these lands and markets alone amounted to 765,000 *dīnars* during the time of 'Abd al-Raḥmān III.[8] Some rulers showed due consideration to the tax-payers when they suffered from any natural calamity. 'Abd al-Raḥmān III on his accession to the throne abolished all illegal taxes. Hakam II reduced the military and extraordinary taxes by one-sixth in 975 A.D. and Hishum II, a year after abolished the tax on olive oil raised in Cordova.[9] The weak and petty rulers confiscated property bequeathed to mosques and Ibn Hazm (d. 1064) expressed disgust at the imposition of heavy and illegal taxes on the Andalusians by the petty rulers of his time.[10]

---

1. Ibn Bassam, *Dhakhirah*, III, p. 100
2. Idrisi, p. 196/239tr; Himyari, p. 162
3. Lopez, *Contribuciones*, p. 91
4. *El Tratado de Ibn 'Abdun*, p. 105
5. *Akhbar Majmu'ah*, 22ff
6. *Islamic Culture*, 1960, pp. 22-27
7. Ibn 'Idhari, II, pp. 213, 221/329, 340 tr.
8. *Ibid.* p. 247; *Azhar*, II, p. 27
9. Gayangos, II, p. 134; Ibn 'Idhari, II, 276; *Spanish Islam*, pp. 386, 466, 514
10. Lopez, pp. 110-11; *Al-Andalus*, II, 1934, pp. 36-37/42-43 tr.

Public and Relief works:—A considerable portion of state revenue was spent on the development of the country and on public and relief works. 'Abd al-Raḥmān II spent a large sum on building palaces, mosques and bridges. During the time of 'Abd al-Raḥmān III one-third of the State revenue was spent on the construction of public buildings throughout the empire.[1] Hakam II spent lavishly "in the construction of mosques, houses of reception for the poor, hospitals for the sick and colleges for the youth and he ornamented his capital as well as other large cities in his dominions with baths, inns, markets, fountains and other works of public utility."[2]

During the time of famine, the collection of taxes from peasants was partly suspended. At the time of failure of the crops, due allowance was made by the landlords and the cultivators received compensation for their losses.[3] Distribution of alms became common and royal granary was thrown open for distribution of corn among the famine-stricken people. In 914 A.D. when a severe famine broke out in the country, 'Abd al-Raḥmān III instructed his Prime Minister Badr b. Aḥmad to take special care of the people and, accordingly, the distribution of alms increased under the supervision of the officials of ḥ*isbah*.[4] In the famine relief work of 988-9 A.D. the royal granary of Hajib al-Manṣūr in which he took great pride and which contained four years back 2,000,000 *mudds* of wheat was emptied.[5]

Army:—There were four categories of armies, a permanent army of mercenaries with its headquarters at Cordova, a regular force (*Jund*, mobilised army) organised by the military fief-holders, the irregular soldiers (the *Baladis*), the descendants of the 'Arabs, who had come with Mūsā, and temporary contingent of volunteers (*Hashid*, recruits), enrolled at the time of an expedition.[6]

In the beginning, the soldiers were given fiefs instead of cash salaries and the Syrian *junds* were got settled in different parts of

1. Gayangos, II, 124, 146
2. *Ibid.*, 172
3. Levi-Provencal, *Histoire*, III, 269-70
4. Ibn 'Idhari, II, 173
5. Ibn al-Khatib, *A'mal al-A'lam*, p. 115
6. *Cf.* S. M. Imamudin, *Some Aspects of the Socio-Economic and Cultural Histovy of Muslim Spain*, Leiden, 1965, pp. 60-65

the country. Of the Syrian soldiers about, 7,000 in number under Balj ibn Bis͟hr made the Governor of Spain, Abu'l K͟haṭṭār (743-5 A.D.), settle them in districts, which were granted to them in fief in lieu of their military service.[1] The tribe was the unit of military organization. Sometimes the selection of a commander from a particular tribe or from the neo-Muslims led to confusion in the camp and ultimate defeat of the Muslims in battle, as happened in the battle of Alhandega (*al-K͟handaq*) during the time of 'Abd al-Raḥmān III.

The army organization underwent many changes as the Umayyad Amīrs and K͟halīfahs became more dependent on foreign troops and Hajib al-Manṣūr completed the system introduced by 'Abd al-Raḥmān I, who had built up an army of 40,000 mercenary soldiers mostly Berbers. Hakam I constructed magazines, devised new weapons, kept a permanent force of mercenaries (*ḥas͟ham*) and of guards (*hawas͟hī*) posted at the gate of the palace. He had a standing force of 50,000 Mamluks.[2] They were called *al-Haras* (the guards) and they were all Berbers, Christians and Negroes. They had two large barracks with stables for their horses and two thousand cavalrymen always kept guard on the banks of the Guadalquivir with twenty officers, called *'Arīfs*, in charge of 100 men each.[3] In order to lead expeditions against Galicia, Muḥammad b. 'Add al-Raḥmān II made the military service compulsory for the Cordovans. The number of regular soldiers was raised to 150,000 and of irregular troops to an unlimited number by 'Abd al-Raḥmān III. His bodyguard numbered 12,000 veterans of whom 8,000 were cavalrymen.

The Turks in the East had their counterparts in Spain in the *Saqalibah* (Slavs). A janissary was made of slaves from many nations and races, epecially Slavs. These slaves were mostly brought from Slavonic countries and other parts of Europe by pirates and Jewish slave dealers mainly of Verdun. Like the Turks at Bag͟hdād the Slavs rose to positions of distinction at Cordova. To curtail the military power of the 'Arab tribes, the regimental system was introduced by 'Abd al-Raḥmān III who considered the Slavs

1. *Cf.* Ibn Idhari, *al-Bayan*, II, pp. 33-4/48-9 tr.
2. Ibn 'Idhari, II, p. 81; Nuwayri, p. 195
3. *Cf. Akhbar Majmu'ah*, pp. 129-30

more reliable than 'Arab nobles of Spain. The foreign recruits had been gradually disbanded and native recruits were substituted by Hakam II. This militia degenerated under the command of Ghālib. In order to capture power and to counter Ghālib, Hājib al-Manṣūr removed the native soldiers and unreliable 'Arab officers and recruited more and more the Berber and Christian mercenaries. The Berber soldiers were of two categories: the first consisted of regulars enrolled as soldiers called *murtaziqa*, the second of volunteers called *muttawi'a*.[1] The first had a share in the booty and the second only received prizes and gratuities on victory.

A corps of troops consisting of 5,000 soldiers was under the command of a general called *Amīr* with a big flag (*rayah*). It was divided into five contingents of 1,000 each under the command of an officer called *qa'id* with a flag (*'alam*). Each contingent was divided into five groups of 200 men each, under the command of a *naqib*, with a standard (*liwa'*). Again each group was divided into five sections of 40 men, each commanded by an *'arif* with a band. Each section was finally divided into five squads of 8 men, each under the charge of a *nazīr* with a pennon (*'uqdah*) on his lance.[2] For the inspection of the army an officer called *Sahib al-ard* was appointed by Hājib al-Manṣūr.[3] Expeditions, either to conquer fresh lands or to collect taxes, were normally led in summer, called *Sa'ifah* and very rarely in winter (*Shitayah*).

Tartūshi, a famous scholar of the 6th century hijrah, describes, as an eye witness, an engagement between the Spanish Muslims and the Christians thus: The Muslim foot soldiers, armed with shields, long lances and provided with sharp pointed javelins, constituted the first row. They put their lances obliquely on their shoulders, the base touching the earth and the point facing the enemy. They put their left knee on the ground raisiug the shield in the front. The archers were in the second row with pointed arrows which were capable of piercing coats of mail. Behind them was drawn up the cavalry in the third row. When the attack began none of those who were kneeling down abandoned their position until

1. Ibn 'Idhari, *al-Bayan*, III, p. 39
2. Levi-Provencal, *L' Espagne*, p. 141
3. *Ibid*., p. 142

the enemy came within range. Then the archers shot their arrows and the foot soldiers threw their javelins and met the enemy with the points of their lances. The infantry and archery then moved towards the right and left leaving in the middle a passage through which the cavalry charged the advancing foe and inflicted a defeat on the enemies if God so desired.[1]

For the payment of the soldiers there was a military *Dıwan* and towards the later part of the Umayyad rule there was introduced a *Malahiq al-Diwan* to pay the auxiliary force.[2] The Syrian junds served in the army for three months at a stretch and received 200 dinars, while the 'Arab *Baladis* served for six months and received 100 dinars. The Syrians were exempt from the payment of tithes (*'Ushr*), while the *Baladis* paid tithes like other subjects. There was a third group of Syrians and 'Arabs who participated in expeditions on the same conditions as other subjects did.[3] The regular soldiers, excluding 'Arab *Baladis*, received additional pay at the end of each campaign at the rate of five to ten dinars per head.[4] Throughout the 9th century cash payment and feudatory systems overlapped one another. In the 10th century feudatory system was totally abolished and soldiers were paid in cash which increased the military efficiency and state expenditure considerably.[5]

Navy:—In the beginning the Umayyad Amīrs did not pay much attention to the improvement of the navy and this was one of the main reasons for their failure to extend their empire beyond the Pyrenees. It was only when the Normans plundered the coastal towns and Seville that 'Abd al-Raḥmān II fortified the coastal areas and established a coast-guard. He got the demolished *mīnar*, which guided the sailors to the Andalusian coasts, repaired.[6] In order to guard Ceuta and Gibraltar 'Abd al-Raḥmān II posted a fleet manned by mariners and soldiers under the command of two *Qa'ids*, Aḥmad b. Muḥammad b. Ilyās and Yūnus b. Sa'īd on the African coast in 931 A.D.[7] A quarter of

1. Alarcon, *Lampara de los principes*, II, Madrid, 1931, pp. 332-3; R. Levy, *Sociology of Islam*, II, p. 340
2. Levi-Provencal, *L' Espagne*, 129
3. Levi-Provencal, *L' Espagne*, pp. 132-3
4. *Cf. Cambridge Medieval History*, III, p. 431
5. *Cf.* Levi-Provencal, *L' Espagne*, pp. 135-6
6. *The Ta'rikh-i-Fath Unduis*, p. 67
7. Ibn 'Idhari, *al-Bayan*, II, 220/340 tr.

a century later the Caliph sent another fleet under the command of a *Saḥib al-Shurtah*, Ahmad b. Ya'la.[1] The Spanish navy, with Pechina or Almeria as its chief naval base, became the most powerful in the Mediterranean Sea. The navy of 'Abd al-Rahmān III disputed the supremacy of the Western Mediterranean Sea with the Fātimid fleet and in 953 A.D. destroyed a Sicilian ship bound for Mahdiyah. 'Abd Allāh b. Riyāhin was the *qa'id al-Bahr* during the time of 'Abd al-Rahmān III as well as Hakam II. Naval workshops were established at Tortosa, Denia, Alicante, Almeria, Vera, Algeciras, Iviza, Saltes, Silves and Santa Maria. Along the banks of the Guadalquivir there were important shipyards for building and repairing ships called *marsa* and *dar-al-Sana* a word which passed into European languages, Spanish *atarazana* and English 'arsenal.'

In 1116-7 Abu al-Salat Umayyah b. 'Abd al-'Azīz of Spain visited Egypt and made an attempt for salvaging a ship. The submerged ship was brought out but sank again because the silken tow-rope broke under the strain.[2]

Generally an Andalusian ship took 36 days to reach the Syrian coast. In 1182-3 Ibn Jubayr, a famous Andalusian sailor, travelled in a Genoese ship from Andalusia to Alexandria in 20 days.[3]

There were two kinds of naval officers, e.g., high officials called *ru'asa'* and low officials, *aṣhab al-arjud*. Every warship was under the command of a qā'id, captain, who occupied himself with equipment, training of the sailors, and manning of the vessels. The second officer, *ra'īs*, was put in charge of navigation The crew of the ship included *nakhuda* (the master), *ruhban* or *rahban* (captain), *didban* (inspector or lookout man) and others.

In the beginning the Muslim sailors dreaded very much the furrowing of the rough and stormy waters of the Atlantic Ocean. In order to attack Galicia from the coast a fleet of boats under the command of 'Abd al-Hamīd ibn Mughīth sailed down the river Guadalquivir in 879 A.D. and reached the Atlantic Ocean but it was dispersed completely by a storm.[4] About one hundred

1. Ibn 'Idhari, *al-Bayan*, II, 238/368-9
2. Sulayman Nadvi, *Arbon ki Jahazrani*, 169
3. Gibb, *Rihlat Ibn Jubair*, pp. 35-38
4. *Ibn 'Idhari, al-Bayan*, II, 106-7; Nuwayri, p. 56/48-9 tr.

and eighteen years later a sizeable fleet was fitted out at Qaṣr Abī Dānish and launched a successful attack on Galicia.[1] By the 10th century the Muslim sailors of Lisbon began to explore the extent of the Atlantic Ocean and discover the other shore. Thus an unsuccessful attempt was made by a party of eight sailors. About two-and-a-half centuries later another Spanish sailor, Ibn Fāṭimah, travelled along the Atlantic coast of Africa and wrote about the interior of Africa. These stories of Muslim adventures in the Atlantic Ocean prove undoubtedly that the western coast of Africa was known to the Spanish Muslim sailors and suggest that perhaps by this route they might have gone to the southern and eastern coasts of Africa and also that they might have known the sea route across the Indian Ocean even before Vasco da Gama's voyage in 1498. According to 'Arab and Portuguese traditions, the Arabs showed Vasco da Gama the route to India and supplied him with a chart of the sea-route known to the Mediterranean sailors. It was thus that the Muslim spirit of discovery of new lands and new waters ultimately enabled the Portuguese to land on the Indo-Pakistani sub-continent and to discover the Americas.[2]

1. Gayangos, II, p. 194
2. *Cf.* S. M. Imamuddin, *Some Aspects of the Socio-Economic and Cultural History of Muslim Spain*, Leiden, 1965, 70-71 :

CHAPTER V

ADMINISTRATION UNDER THE FATIMIDS

Fatimid Khilafat:—According to the Sunni traditions Prophet Muḥammad had not provided for an heir but the Shi'ahs believed in the progeny of the Prophet and his descendants were lawful rulers after him. Whereas the companions of the Prophet insisted upon election according to seniority, the party favouring Hadrat 'Alī advocated a system of hereditary appointment within 'Alī's family.

The Mu'tazalah and Isma'iliyah sects were the oldest in Islām to reconcile religion with philosophy. Although the Isma'ilis, according to many, have based their teachings on the principles of the Mu'tazalites whose founder was Wāṣil b. 'Atā (d. 81 H./700 A.D.), Isma'ilis like other Shi'ite sects believe that Hadrat 'Alī is the source of spiritual knowledge and his descendants inherited it from him until it reached Hadrat Imām Ja'far Sādiq (d. 148H/765 A.D.) who preached it widely. According to the Isma'ili tradition, Imām Ja'far Sādiq took special precaution in preaching '*Ulūm Batiniyah* (the knowledge of secret) and it was he who preached the appearance of Mahdī. The Isma'ilī *da'īūn* tried their best to spread Isma'ilism in North Africa eroding the political supremacy of the 'Abbāsids there, the Chief *da'ī* being Abū 'Abd Allāh al-Husain al-Shi'ī a native of San'a' in al-Yaman. In 296H 909 A.D he got Sa'īd al-Mahdī a descendant of the Persian 'Abd Allāh ibn Maymūn released from the prison of Sijilmāsah where he had been retained by the Aghlabid ruler Ziyādat Allāh (903-909) destroying the century-old Aghlabid dynasty and driving out Ziyādat Allāh from al-Maghrib to Palestine and entrusting al-Mahdī with the administration of the newly created State. But he met the same fate which Abū Muslim Khurāsānī did at the hands of the 'Abbāsids in the East.[1]

As religion Isma'ilism was preached in al-Maghrib culminating in politics and after the conquest of some cities Mahdī announced

---

1. *Cf. Jahan Kusha'i Juwaini*, III, p. 150

the freedom of religious belief so that people would accept him as their **Imam**, i.e., secular as well as religious head. The teaching of spiritual faith was limited from now on to the *da'wat* group and the religious age was converted to the political age. Thus was founded a Shi'ite *khilafat* as a rival to the Sunnī Caliphate, the Umayyads of Spain and the 'Abbāsids of Irāq. Although there were three Caliphates ('Abbāsids, Fātimids and Umayyads) when Māwardi wrote he preached that there could not be two *imams* in the community at one and the same time. The Andalusian and the North-African savant who were realistic, however, favoured the legality of there being more than one Caliph at one and the same time provided they were not in one and the same country.[1] Soon the newly created Fātimid State expanded outside al-Maghrib to the Mediterranean islands and Egypt and also the Asiatic lands of Syria and Palestine and the capital shifted first from Raqādah near Qairawān to Mahdiyah, a newly founded city in Tunis and from Mahdiyah again to another newly constructed city of *al-Qahirah* (Cairo) in Egypt.

While the Sunnis believed in the *khilafat* where people had rights to elect and choose their own head, the Shi'ahs believed in the divinely appointed *Imam*, whom, the people, having no other alternative, had to accept as their religious and secular head. According to Māwardi, the *Imamat* or Caliphate was divinely appointed Government of the world in order to defend the faith and establish the right.[2] Obedience to the *Imams* is, therefore, divinely imposed upon the Muslims that they have authority over the latter.[3] The *Imamiyahs* maintain that the head of Islām must be a descendant of Prophet Muḥammad through his daughter Fātimah.

The Fātimids, who claimed their descent from Hadrat Fātimah the daughter of Prophet Muḥammad and wife of Hadrat 'Alī being Shi'ah believed in the *Imamat* of 'Alī who was appointed as his successor, according to the Shi'ah tradition, by Prophet Muḥammad having received instruction to that effect from God Himself.[4]

1. *Cf.* Ibn Khaldun, *Prolegomenes,* Fr. tr. de Slane, I, p. 391
2. *Cf. Al-Ahkam al-Sultaniyah*, ed. by M. Enger, Bonn, 1853
3. *Cf.* Ibn Khaldun, *Prolegomenes*, Fr. tr. de Slane, I, 388
4. Ibn Khaldun, *Prolegomenes*, I, 355; Tr. de Slane, I, p. 400; Shahristani, *Kitab al-Milal*, ed. Custom. pp. 2-3 quoted by R. Levy, *The Social Structure of Islam*, Cambridge 1957, 288n.3

'Abd Allāh al-Mahdī, the founder of the Fātimid State in al-Maghrib, appeared in Qairawān in 297 H/910 A.D. and claimed himself to be a descendant of Hadrat Imām Ja'far al-Sādiq, and as such, the secular and spiritual head of the Shi'ah Muslims. Like the Ummayyad and 'Abbāsid Caliphs he preached in the mosque, presided over the divine service, decided religious and secular disputes and acted as a temporal sovereign in all other respects. Thus his hereditary *Imamat* or *Khilafat* continued in the Fātimid State and Hākim, son of 'Azīz, became Caliph even when he was only eleven years old, 'Mustansir became Caliph while he was only seven years of age and Āmir sat on the *masnad* of *Khilafat* at the age of five and on his death his two and a half years old son Tayy became Caliph but he was kept concealed by the *da'is* because of the fear of enemies.

During the infancy of an *Imam* or Caliph he was assisted by his *kafil* or *mustawda'* in his religious and state functions, which often created complications as he was opposed sometimes by his *walī* or *wazīr*. Both the sons of Imām Mustanṣir the elder, Nazar, and the younger, Must'ali, claimed himself to be the *Imam* bringing ruin to the Fātimid dynasty and the Shi'ite State. Like the Sassanid Kings the Fātimid Caliphs were fond of pomp and grandeur and their display in public. They introduced the convention of their subjects' bowing down before them. Hākim, however, stopped this Roman practice.

Central Administration :—To administer the State the Fātimid Caliph established an assembly called *da'wat* consisting of several *arkan* (departments). We have a sketch of the details of the Fātimid military and civil administrative organs from the pen of Qalqashandī (d. 822/1419) and Maqrīzī (d. 846H/1442 A.D.), the two contemporary writers of Egypt.[1]

There were two kinds of officials, one of which was close to the *Khalīfah* and posted at the capital and another member of which was called *walī* and posted in the provinces. The central officials (courtiers) were divided into four classes.

The First Class official consisted of the 'men of the sword'

1. *Cf* Zahid 'Ali, *Ta'rikh-i-Fatimi' in Misr*, Vol. II, 1963, pp. 99-103.

consisting again of two sub-classes of which one was that of the common soldiery having nine officials and the other was that of *kẖwajah sara* (eunuchs) also consistiag of nine *muhtamim*.

Wazarat :-- The *wazīr* was the chief of all officials and he came sometimes from the 'men of the sword', and at other times from the 'men of the pen.' The office next to the *wazarat* was called *wasatat* having lesser rights than the *wazarat*. Ya'qūb ibn Killis the financial Chief of Mu'izz was the first *wazīr* in the Fatimid Egypt appointed by 'Azīz b'illah in 363/973-4. He was *wazir Tanfidh* with limited power to mediate between 'Azīz and his officials. After Ibn Killis, the person who held this office until the time of Hākim was called *sahib wasatat* or *safarat*. From the time of Zāhir, the office of *wazīr* began to function again and they were from among the 'men of the pen.' From the days of Badr al-Jamālī until the fall of the Fātimid *Kẖilafat* all those who became *wazīr* were from among the 'men of the sword.' The *wazīr* had a special type of rich official dress having gold buttons and jewels. A golden inkpot inlaid with jewels was fixed on the stirrup of his riding animal which was normally a donkey.[1] Like his Bagẖdād colleague, the *wazīr* drew a monthly salary of 5,000 *dīnars* although the salaries of other official heads and ministers were much smaller.[2]

Although the Fatimids are known for borrowing their religious, social and political ideas from Persia, yet the institution of the *wazarat* in the Shi'ite Caliphate of the Fātimids was less significant than it was in the Sunni Caliphate of the 'Abbāsids. It achieved importance only towards the end of the reign of al-Mu'izz. The early Fātimid Caliphs administered the country with the help of executive officers who had no delegated powers but carried out the orders and instructions of the Caliph. To supervise the collection of *Kẖaraj*, and other related financial matters, men like 'Abd Allāh b. al-Qadim of Banī Agẖlab, the chief executive officer, and Abū Ja'far Muḥammad b. Aḥmad al-Bagẖdādī were appointed in different capacities under 'Ubayd Allāh al-Mahdī (296-322/909-934). In the absence of Mu'izz when Jawhar the Sicilian slave by origin (d. 381H/991) conquered Egypt he had to act as a representative

1. *Cf.* Maqrizi, *Khitat*, II, p. 309; Qalqashandi, *Subh-al-A'sha*, III, 490
2. *Cf.* Maqrizi, *Itti'az al-Hunafa* (ed. Shayyal), p. 78

executive officer without having delegated authority.[1] The Qā'id Jawhar appointed the Ikhshid Ibn al-Furāt as the Fātimid *wazir* in Egypt under his own supervision in order to soothe the Egyptian Sunni feelings.[2]

Al-Mu'izz outlined his political and religious policy to be followed in his farewell speech to his troops consisting of Kutāmah (Kitāmah) tribesmen laying stress on the principle of justice and following his master, the Qa'id al-Jawhar outlined his sagacious policy of religious toleration, justice, peace and pacification while granting peace and directed gradual replacement of the native and orthodox officials with trained Fātimid administrators. On the arrival of Mu'izz in Egypt he surrendered all his offices in the administration except that of the commander-in-chief of the army. Ibn al-Furāt resigned from office in 363H/974 A.D. but he was re-appointed *wazir* twice under al-'Azīz.[3]

In other words, during the early period of the Fātimid rule (909-1074 A.D.), there functioned *wazarat tanfidh* known as *wasatat* or *safarat* in the Fātimid terminology identical to 'Abbāsid executive ministry.[4] Such ministers or officials were selected largely from *arbab al-qalam* (men of the pen) e.g. civilians. The first man to be addressed as *wazīr* was Ya'qūb ibn Killis (d. 380H//220 A.D.) a Jewish convert, minister of al-'Aziz. He was a very learned man and an author of reputation. His lectures were attended by the judges, theologians and poets every Friday night. Badr al-Jamālī was the first military person to hold the post of *wazīr* under al-Mustanṣir (1035-1095) in 1074 A.D. It antagonised the civilians but proved the weakness of the Fātimid Caliph whose power was now shared for the first time in the Fātimid history by his *wazīr al-tafwīd* with delegated powers in adverse circumstances created by the revolts of the Turkish soldiers.[5] Badr al-Jamālī was commander-in-chief of the armies as well as director of civil administration and in the latter capacity he often appointed the Chief *Qadī* and other dignitaries of the State.[6]

1. Mez, *Renaissance*, p. 23
2. Maqrizi, *Itti'az*, pp. 79, 85 quoted by Vatikiotis, p. J., *The Fatimid Theory of State*, Lahore, 1957, p. 97
3. Maqrizi, *Itti'az*, pp. 137-8, 148-53 and Ibn Hammad, *Akhbar al-Muluk*, Paris, 1927, pp. 41-44; Vatikiotis, pp. 142-43
4. Qalqashandi, *Subh al-A'sha*, Cairo, 1913, III, pp. 489-90
5. Ibn Muyassar, *Akhbar Misr*, pp. 5-7 quoted by Vatikiots, p. 97
6. Maqrizi, *Khitat*, I, 440; Qalqashandi, III, 482-3

Al-Mustanṣir had recalled Badr al-Jamālī from Acre in 466H/1074 A.D. while the Sunni Turks were in revolt. He was an extreme Shi'ah. He suppressed the Turks and restored order in appreciation of which he was delegated practically with all authorities in the State and after him his son al-Afdal enjoyed the same power and prestige. The latter even appointed his own caliph in preference to the heir-designate of Mustanṣir's eldest son.[1] From the time of Badr al-Jamālī, the institution of *wazarat* in Egypt became synonymous and identical with that of the 'Abbāsids and the post of *wazīr* was filled by various military men infuriating a leading, *da'ī al-Mu'ayyad fi al-Din* to the point of writing to *wazīr* al-Yazuri of al-Mustanṣir for the restoration of *wazarat* to 'men of letters.'[2] Thenceforward the *wazīr* used to be a soldier and generally entitled *amīr al-juyush* (commander of the armies) instead of *wazir*. As the days passed on the Fātimid Caliphs became weak and their *wazīrs* strong and the latest *wazīrs* were called *Malik* (King) in addition to their having other titles. In 530/1136 Ridwān ibn Walakhshi received the titles of *al-Sayyid al-Ajalī*, *al-Malik al-Afdal* (the most distinguished lord and the most excellent king) from the Fātimid Caliph al-Hāfiẓ.[3]

Sahil al-Bab (Lord of the Gate) was next to the *wazīr* and called sometimes as *wazīr asghar* or *wazīr adna*. Besides performing his palace duties, he had the privilege of presenting ambassadors before the Fātimid Caliphs. There were assistant lords of doors who looked after the interest of the ambassadors and held their left hands while presenting them before the Fātimid Caliph while the lord of doors had the privilege of holding their right hands.

Army:—*Al-Qa'id* (commander-in-chief) led the army and was responsible for the protection of the Caliph's Palace. The army consisted of three principal ranks:

(a) *Umara'* were divided into three sub-ranks: (*i*) *umara' mutawwaqīn* having golden chain round the neck received *khil'at* from the Caliph, (*ii*) silver sword bearers who accompanied the Caliph riding on horseback and (*iii*) ordinary *umara'*;

---

1. *Cf.* Ibn Khaldun *Kitab al-'Ibar*, IV, pp. 64-66; Maqrizi, *Khitat*, I, 408-9; *Cf.* Vatikiotis, p. 167
2. *Cf. Al-Sirat al-Mu'ayyadiya*, pp. 89-94 quoted by Vatikiotis, 96
3. Maqrizi, *Khitat*, I, 440; Levy, p. 387

(*b*) Royal body-guards consisting of (*i*) *ustad* or *khwajah sara*, 1,000 in number whose officers were called *muhnakin*; (*ii*) Special young guards 5,000 in number; and (*iii*) Ordinary young guards 5,000 in number; they were like the eunuchs readily available for service and called *jaisan al-hujar* because they lived in small rooms (*hujrah*) built for them;

(c) the different regiments named after a caliph or a *wazīr* or a nationality, as Hāfiẓiyah, Āmiriyah, Juyūshiyah, Afdaliyah, Sudaniyah, Rumiyah, Turkiyah, Kurdiyah, Dalamiyah. Every regiment had an officer to look after it.

The *Dīwan al-Jaysh wa'l-Rawatib* (the Department of Army and Emoluments) besides being an army pay-office maintained muster-rolls, list of soldiers in active service, record of military fiefs etc.

Before the conquest of Egypt the Fātimids had their soldiers mostly from the Kutāmah tribe of the Berbers in al-Maghrib but after its conquest they paid less attention to the West as it was diverted to the East and when they conquered Syria and Asia Minor they found a new region and people (the Dalmite and the Turkish slaves) for the recruitment of soldiers. Among the new recruits the number of the Turks began to increase fast. This led to rivalry between the Kutāmahs and the Turks and to the trial of their strength on the death of al-'Aziz. To balance the strength of the Berbers specially the Kutamahs in the army al-'Aziz ordered Ya'qub b. Killis for the purchase of Dalmite and Turkish slaves and for their recruitment in the army and thus with Aftakin Turkish regiment of the royal prisons was raised.[1] As his son and successor Hākim was only eight years of age the entire power in the state vested with his guardian and tutor, Barjwān leader of the Turkish faction who was a good singer and treasurer and Amīr Hasan bin Ammār, the commander of the Berber troops who cared little for the interest of the Fatimid Caliphate.[2] In the terrible conflict that took place between these two leaders and their factions, Ibn Ammār succeeded and Barjwān was removed from the administration reducing his hold on Hakim's palace only as his personal guard.

1. *Cf.* '*Uyun al-Akhbar*. VI, p. 192
2. Cf. Ibn al-Athir, IX, p. 49

Ibn 'Ammār assumed power and adopted the title of *Amīn-al-Dawlah* with a view to establish a secular state setting aside the Caliph. Hākim, therefore, encouraged Barjwān to regain his position with the alliance of Manjutakin the Turkish governor of Syria. Ibn Ammār occupied Syria and transferred Barjwān's Turkish supporters to Cairo. There they revolted in 390H/1000 A.D. Ibn 'Ammār was deposed and killed. Barjwān came to power and the rise of the Turks in the army was now completed with the gradual decline of the Berbers. This led to the Berbers' revolt under their governor Mansūr b. Yūsuf bin Bulkin in al-Maghrib. They were suppressed temporarily but from then onwards they became autonomous with their nominal attachment with the Fātimid Khilāfat. The defeat of the Kutamahs whose ancestors had been the backbone of the Fatimid dynasty became the cause of the ruin of the dynasty. Under Mustanṣir Berber's strength in the army was reduced to one-fourth.[1] Under the influence of Mustanṣir's mother an Abyssinian about one-fourth of the army was formed of the Abyssinian slaves. Under Mustanṣir the Sudani slaves alone were 10,000 in number. Their mutual jealousy brought later Badr Jamali from Syria to form a new corps of Armenian soldiers in Egypt giving a final blow to the Berbers.[2]

The Fātimids had a strong navy stationed in the naval ports of Ifriqiyah, Egypt and Syria. The navy was important both for military as well as for commercial purposes. The second Fātimid capital, Mahdiyah, was primarily a naval base It controlled the Mediterranean islands. The Syrian and Egyptian ports were soon developed into strategic naval bases; Iskandariyah, Fayyūm, Dimiyāt, 'Asqalan, Akkah (Acre), Suwar, 'Aydhāb and others each having at least an armada of seventy-five boats, ten *mustahat* and ten *ṣamalat* under an *amīr al-bahr*.[3] The Fatimids controlled the East-West trade route through the Mediterranean and the Red Seas which made it entirely independent of the Abbasid *Khilafat*.

The naval strength of Mu'izz was so high that the Mediterranean water from Sicily to the Syrian excluding the northern limits of the Sea was controlled by the Fatimids whose rivals were only

1. Zahid 'Ali, I, 285-6
2. *Ibid*., I, 306; Jurji Zaidan, I, 232
3. Zahid 'Ali, II, p. 100

the Umayyads of Spain who extended their sphere of influence in the western parts of the Mediterranean Sea and sailed their ships freely and if and when required with the help of arms.

The Fatimids had their ship-building factory at Alexandria and Dimiyat and inside Egypt on the Nile. Among the war ships that they constructed were S͟hunah, Harâfah, Tarâwah and 'Is͟hāriat.[1] Maqs on the Nile was known for the construction of warships and the Nile ships to furrow on the Nile carrying goods and passengers. The naval strength of the Fatimids rose to 5,000. There was an officer over each ten and each receiving ten to twenty dīnars a month. Some soldiers received only two dirhams a month.[2] The navy men received fiefs also besides the usual salary which were called Abwāb G͟hāzī. The chief naval officer was called *Ra'īs* who was acompanied by an *Amir al-Bahr* at the time of an expedition. To encourage them the Caliph himself sometimes distributed salaries and prizes[3] There were 16,000 warships under Mu'izz[4] and after him the naval rtrength started declining till there were left only 100 ships in a Fatimid armada (*astal*). There were fixed *manjaniqs* on the warships which conducted their exercise in the Nile near Caliph's palace at Maqs on the Nile outside Cairo. When the exercise was over the Caliph paid 100 dīnars to the *Muqaddam* and 20 dīnars to the *Ra'is*[5]

Other officials :—There were four other officials at the centre who, although less in importance, were *ṣahib al-mizallah* (bearer of umbrella, swords and lances) and *rikabīyah* (bearer of arms) 2,000 in number under twelve officials accompanying the *Khalifan* while he was out. The fifth and sixth were *walīs* (Governors) of Cairo and Fustāt (Miṣr). The governor of Cairo was a very big official in status and had a special privileged position in the Caliph's retinue.[6]

The other office which belonged to the 'men of the sword' was that of the eunuchs (*ustad* or *khwaja sara'*) called *muhnakin* which

1. *Ta'rikh Tamaddun*, p. 265
2. Jurji Zaidan, I, p. 261
3. *Ibid.*, p 262
4. Jurji Zaidan, *Ta'rikh Misr al-Hadith*, p. 296
5. *Ibid.*, pp. 264-65
6. *Ibid.*, 101

also consisted of nine *muhtamims*, organiser of Caliph's court, in charge of the Caliph's *farman* and who mediated between the Caliph and the *wazir* and were also in charge of the palaces, the treasury, offices and the royal inkpot, a golden inkpot which was inlaid with jewels and fixed on the stirrup of the Caliph's horse, also in-charge of the Caliph's relatives and the *muhtamim* of the kitchen. There were other *khwajah sara'* besides the eunuchs who looked after the descendants of Hadrat 'Alī and arrested those who made false claim of being *Talibi* (descendants of 'Ali). There were also other *khwajah sara'* to look after the interest of different regiments.

The Department of Religious Affairs :—The civil officers belonged to the second class and they were 'men of the pen' attached with the three departments of religious affairs, revenue and technicians (*ahl sana'at*). The Department of religious affairs had six officials at the centre *qadī al-quddat, da'i al-du'at, muhtasib, wakīl bayt al-mal*, assistant lord of the door and the *qari* who recited the *Qura'n.*

Justice:—The *qadī al-quddat* was the chief justice and in-charge of the mint possessing wide powers. As long as the Caliph was strong the *qadī* was appointed by him but when the real power in the state passed to the *wazīr*, he was appointed by the latter.[1] He held office every Saturday and Tuesday in the 'Amir's Mosque (Jāmi' al-'Atīq), on a raised dais with four *vakils* seated in front of him while the witnesses had their seats on the right and left sides of the *qadī*. There were five *hujjabs* in the court. The *qadī* rode on mules with silver stirrups and received a gold embroidered dress as *khil'at.*[2]

The da'ī al-Du'at :—The *da'ī al-du'at* was the chief propagandist. He answered questions on matters of law and religious doctrines and elucidated difficult passages of the *Qura'n.*[3] He presided in the *Daru'l 'Ilm* the institution of Liberary-cum-University and bureau of information and in *Aywan al-Kabīr* and the *Majlis al-Da'ī* the Assembly of propaganda. The office of *da'ī* was hereditary in the family of the Banū 'Abd al-Qawi. He delivered lecture

1. Maqrizi, *Khitat*, I, 403-4
2. Zahid 'Ali, II, 101-2
3. Maqrizi, I, 391

on the faith and belief of *Ahl Bayt* and took oaths of fealty from the newly converted Ismā'ilis.[1]

The early Fatimid Caliphs themselves administered justice with the help of the *da'īs* whose duty since the establishment of the Fātimid *Khilafat* had become two-fold : religious propaganda against the Sunni system of *Khilafat* and to assist the Caliph in administering the newly-born state. On the arrival of Mu'izz in Egypt the *da'wa* affairs were jointly controlled by Abū Hanīfah Muḥammad b. Nu'mān commonly known as Qādin Nu'mān (d. 362H/974) highly esteamed for his learning and justice having no equal in 'Iraq and Egypt and Jaf'ar b. Manṣūr al-Yaman the *Bab al Abwab* of Mu'izz (d. 365H/976). Gradually Qādī Nu'mān concentratėd on judicial matters and Ja'far on the purely religious and organizational affairs of the *da'wa*. Ja'far wrote many authentic works on Isma'ili religion and a book on *zakat* called *Tawil al-Zakat.*[2] Abū Tāhir (al-Dhuhli) Muḥammad b. Aḥmad b. 'Abd Allāh the previous Qādī of Egypt who had helped in the Fātimid conquest of Egypt was retained nominally as the *Qadī al-Quddat* but the main power vested with Nu'mān who had advised the first four Caliphs of the Fātimids in all matters of law and justice and had accompanied Mu'izz to Egypt.[3] To listen to the complaints against governors and other officials a court of appeal under the name of *Adalat Azalah Shikayat* was instituted at Cairo by Jawhar (d. 373/983-4) attended by himself, a minister and *da'is* and orders were passed under his signature.[4]

The official Fatimid law newly instituted in Egypt was mostly based on the Māliki. law which was prevalent in Egypt and al-Maghrib with the variations of Isma'ilism added to it from time to time as and when occasion arose as it is apparent from the classic Fātimid law book *Da'im al-Islam* composed by Nu'mān. Being an encyclopaedic author, historian and jurist he also composed *al-Arjuzah al-Muntakhabah* another book on law composed in poetry.[5]

1. Maqrizi, *Khitat*, I, 458-9
2. Zahid 'Ali, II, 108-109
3. *Cf.* Jurji Zaidan, I, 309-310; O' Leary, *Fatimids of Egypt*, p. 103
4. Jurji Zaidan, I, 309-310
5. Zahid 'Ali, *Ta'rikh Fatimi'in Misr*, II, Karachi, 1963, pp. 109-110; *Cf.* 'Abbas Hamdani, *The Fatimids*, Karachi, 1962, p. 20

His sons 'Ali (d. 374H/984-5) and Abu 'Abd Allah Muḥammad (d.389H/999 A.D.), and grandson Abū 'Abd Allāh Husain (d. 395/1005) held the post of chief justice in succession. Muḥammad Nu'mān surpassed all in learning and justice. During his time under Caliph 'Aziz, Imām Mālik's *Muwattan* was banned, *Salat al-Tarawiḥ* was stopped in 372/982-3 and much stress was laid on Ismā'ili theology although Māliki School the only Sunni School was also recognised by the courts of justice under the Fatimids.

To judge cases relating to complaints against the public officers the Fatimid Caliph himself administered justice in the court of the *Mazalim* (the highest court of appeal) but during their decaying period the *wazir* or the *Sahib al-bab* reviewed such cases sitting at the golden gate of the palace in Cairo.[1] He was assisted by the chief representaives of the various communities and the chamberlains and also a crier to summon parties. The complaints were confirmed by the Caliph and copied by the scribe and handed over to the petitioner by the chamberlain at the palace gate.[2]

Hisbah :—The *Muḥtasib*, who was the magistrate of the capital and prefect of the Fatimid State, co-ordinated the departments of police and justice and kept watch on roads, markets and other public places and looked after sale and purchase, weights and measures, cheats and culprits and public morals and inflicted punishments on the spot.

Police :—The Fatimids continued the old policing system in Egypt having two types—civilian and military police and appointed trusted Isma'ilī followers to the post of *Sahib al-Shurtah* and his staff mostly from al-Maghrib the recruiting ground for soldiers. The *Sahib al-Shurtah* was at one and the same time the head of the royal bodyguard and chief of the police force (*Shurtah*) of the capital and provincial towns. This post was held by one of al-Zahir's ministers.[3] The *Shurtah* department was very strong under the Fatimids and exercised some of the powers of the *qadī* in listening to the complaints against offences, religious and social, and in dispensing justice.[4]

1. *Cf. Bulletin de L' Institut Francais d'Archeologie public sous le direction de M. George Foucart*, Tome XXVI, Cairo 1926 and Margoliouth, *Cairo, Jerusalem and Damascus*, pp. 22-3 quoted by Fatima Sadique, *S., Baybars I of Egypt*, Dacca 1956, pp. 114-5
2. Maqrizi, *Khitat*, I, 402-3; Levy, pp. 350-51
3. *Ibid.*, pp. 354, 402-3
4. Jurji Zaidan, I, p. 313

Bayt al-Mal :—The *Wakil bayt al-mal* besides performing his presidential duty as treasurer was entrusted with the task of having the slaves liberated and married and also of getting royal palaces and boats constructed. The various departments of the public *Bayt al-mal* were under the control of the *dīwan al-nazr* (ministry of supervision). The chief of the *dīwan* was answerable to the Caliph or the *Wazir* for the function of his department and with whom the ambassadors and governors had to communicate in the first instance.[1] The Assistant Lord of Doors looked after the interest of the ambassadors and held their left hands while presenting them before the Fatimid Caliph and the Lord of Doors had the privilege of holding their right hands.

The *Dīwan al-Majlis* dealt with the privy purse of the civil list, departments of gifts, allowances to royal family members and retainers and also of *iqta'at* (fiefs) granted on the promise of annual return to the treasury.[2] The *wazīr* received 5,000 *dīnars* and other officials like treasurer, the *Sahib al-mizallah* (bearer of the state ambrella) and director of the palace 100 *dīnars* each.[3]

In<u>sh</u>a' :—The *Daftar of In<u>sh</u>a'* (Correspondence) consisted of one *Mu'tamadī* having *mun<u>sh</u>i* experts for making drafts of letters and another two *munshis* (scribes) of the Caliph one to record his order and instruction and another to make it fair. Special attention was paid to this department of *In<u>sh</u>a'* in the Fātimid State.[4] Two of al-Zāhir's ministers had been in charge of the *Diwan al-In<u>sh</u>a'* (the chancery). Both Jews and Christians were generally appointed in this department.

<u>Kh</u>araj :—The Department of Revenue (*Diwan al-<u>Kh</u>araj*) was divided into fourteen sections: one was *Sig<u>h</u>ah al-tahqiq* called *Ras al-dawawin* to keep watch on the workings of other thirteen sections of revenue department each entrusted with a definite assigment like collection of *k<u>h</u>araj*, payment of salaries, distribution of stipends and presents etc.

---

1. Maqrizi, I, 400
2. *Ibid*., 397-8
3. *Ibid*., I, 401; Qalqashandi, III, 492 quoted by Levy, p. 390
4. *Ibid*, II, 246; Cf. for the rules and regulations of *diwan al-rasa'il* Ibn Sairfi's *Ru'asa'ul Kitab fi al-Dawlat al-Fatimiyah* quoted by Zahid 'Ali, II, p. 102

Ya'qūb ibn Killis al-Baghdadi, a Jewish administrator of great reputation in Egypt, due to his differences with the Ikhshids had escaped to al-Maghrib in 357/968 and accepted the post of *Sahib al-kharaj* under Mu'izz. He introduced reforms in the financial administration. Six years after he returned to Egypt in the retinue of the Fātimid army. On the conquest of Egypt the financial chief 'Ali b. Yahyā was retained in his office formally although the real power vested with Ibn Killis. Driving the Abbāsid coins out of circulation Ibn Killis assisted by Asluj al-Hasan introduced Fātimid currency (*Mu'izzi dinars*). Due to his wise financial policy trade and industry develcped, revenue of the country increased and public and religious monuments were constructed bringing prosperity to the Fatimid State.[1] He exercised complete control over revenue and civil administration during the last days of Mu'izz and under 'Aziz.

Among the technicians (*Ahl ṣana'at*) at the centre the physicians held the highest rank. The Caliph's physician had his office near the golden palace of the Caliph's *Qal'at al-Dhahab*. 'Alī al-Hasan ibn al-Haytham (d. 531H/1040) was a renowned court physician of the Fatimid times. His book *Kitab al-Manazirah* on the science of vision influenced the European authors greatly.[2] There were poets both from the Sunnis and Shi'ahs in the Fatimid court. 'Ali b. Husayn of Baghdad was granted 6,000 dinars a year as a political stipend and included in the list of the Fatimid Shaykhs by 'Aziz.[3]

Province :—The Fatimid State of Egypt was divided into four units of administration - Wilāyat Quṣ (Upper Egypt), the greatest division,[4] *Wilayat Sharqiyah*, *Wilayat Gharbiyah* and Wilāyat Iskandriyah. Syria and the territory bordering on Asia Minor formed the other two main divisions of the empire. The *walī* was the chief administrator of the province and was assisted by other provincial officials like the *qadī*, military generals and tax-collectors. In the towns of Syria and Asia Minor native officials who controlled the local officials of the district towns were posted. They were entrusted with local works and recruitment of soldiers for fighting war and labourers for digging new canals and repairing old ones.

1. Zahid 'Ali, II, 103
2. *Ibid.*, II, 113-4
3. Cf. Maqrizi, II, 459
4. *Mu'jam al-Buldan*, IV, p. 201

The *fallahin* (cultivators) received fair and paternal treatment from the Fatimid Caliphs. Skilled labours like supervisors and engineers were appointed under the direct control of the centre for the management of big canals. Special attention was paid to the development of irrigarion and agriculture.[1]

Revenue:—In the 9th century, according to Maqrīzī, two types of revenue were collected in Egypt— *kharaj* collected on products of land annually and *hilalī* tax realised on non-agriculture products on monthly basis for the first time in Egypt by the *walī* of taxes namely Aḥmad b. Muḥammad b. Mudabbir in 250H/864 A.D. The taxes which he imposed on pasture became known as *mara'ī* and those which were realised on river products were called *masa'id*. This *hilali* tax was also known as *marfiaq* and *mu'awin* and collected monthly.[2] *Mukūs* is the plural of *maks* means loss as it was a sale tax and the sellers incurred a loss thereby. The collector of *mukūs* known as *makkas* was hated and despised. The collection of taxes from this source which amounted to one hundred thousand dinars a year and had been stopped by Aḥmad b. Tūlūn, was re-introduced by the later Fātimid rulers. It came to be known as *mukūs* and was again stopped by Salāḥ al-Dīn Ayyūbī.[3] Solar year was followed in the collection of land tax and lunar in that of the *mukūs* duty and *jizyah* which were collected in the month of Muḥarram. The *mukūs* or incidental taxes (*ahdath*) included tolls on drugs, spices, cotton, timber, salt, fish, matting and other merchandise exported or imported. The rent collected from public buildings like flour-mills, slaughter houses, *hammams* and *bazars* also formed part of the *hilali* or *mukūs* revenues.[4]

During the time of Mustanṣir, according to Qādī Ibn Qahhāl (d. 483/1090), taxes collected were 21,040,040 *dinars* from northern province[5] and 1,020,953 from southern onc and, according to Abū Sālih al-Armini al-Naṣrānī, about 60,000 *dīnars* were collected from Alexandria, Dimiyāt, Taft and Naqqādah.[6]

1. Qalqashandi, III, 482-98
2. Maqrizi, I, pp. 103, 107
3. *Ibid*, I, 166-69; Cf. *Ibn Jubayr* (ed. Wright and de Goeje), pp. 39-42.
4. *Ibid.*, I, 103-4, 107
5. Zahid 'Ali, p. 138
6. Lane-Poole, p. 152

Other types of taxes were *zakat*, *khums*, *fitrah*, *najwa* and *jizyah*. *Zakat* was levied on the monetary capital (the minimum limit being 20 *dīnars* or 200 *dīrhams*), live-stock and garden or field produce at the rate of 2½ per cent.[1] *Khums* was one-fifth of the booty as the State share. *Jizyah* was collected from the people of the books (Christians and Jews) at the rate of one and one-third *dīnar* per head during the time of Āmir, and the rate was enhanced by *Wazīr* Ridwān under Hafiẓ to two *dīnars* per head.[2] A special class of *jizyah* was collected from the Armenians in Upper Egypt and Aswān at the rate of a *dīnar* and two *qirats* per head.[3] A new tax was collected under the head of *najwa* by the Fātimids. At the time of accepting the Ismā'ilī faith the followers had to pay three and one-third of a dirham to the *da'ī* or *Imam* as *nadhranah*. Some rich followers preferred to pay thirty-three and two-thirds of a *dīnar*.[4] Besides these taxes the Fātimid Caliph had an important source of income from the city of Cairo. Rent was collected from shops, hotels, bath-rooms and other public buildings. Rent was collected at the rate of two to ten *dīnars* from the shops of Cairo as recorded by Nāṣir Khusraw (d. 1074) amounting to thousands of *dīnars*.[5] The average income from Fustat alone was 50,000 *dinars* and sometimes it rose to 120,000 *dinars*.

Assisted by 'Asluj ibn Hasan, Ya'qub ibn Killis invited contracts(*qabalah*) for the taxes due from private estates and alloted them to those who guaranteed advance payment to the treasury. *Mawat* (dead) lands were given as grants for raising military funds and other public expenditure.[6] Private lands escheated to the crown were also granted as military fiefs enriching a class of officials but impoverishing the peasanrty and turning them to a class of land-slaves attached to the soil.[7]

1. Ibn Mammati, *Kitab al-Qawanin al-Dawawin*, Cambridge 175. fols. 40ff quoted by Levy, p. 392 n1
2. Lane-Poole, p. 152
3. Ibn Mammati, fol. 43b quoted by Levy, p. 392n2
4. Maqrizi, II, 226
5. *Safarnamah-i-Nasir Khusraw*, pp. 127-132
6. Maqrizi, I, 97
7. *Ibid.*, pp. 83, 97; Cf. Poliak, *Feudalism in Egypt, Syria, Palestine and Lebanon*, 33-4

Caliph Hākim noticed that because of the leniency and patronage of 'Azīz the Christian and Jewish financial officials had been corrupt. Having been determined to curb their power he got killed some of them in 393/1003 and imposed restrictions on the use of dress by the Jews and Christians. In 373/983-4 for a few months Ibn Killis fell out of the grace of 'Aziz and was fined 200,000 *dinars*[1] and imprisoned along with the commander Faḍl b. Sālih. A year after he was reinstated to his post and the money confiscated was returned to him. According to Ibn Munjib Sayrafi the annual salary of Ibn Killis was 100,000 *dīnars* equivalent to £50,000[2] and he had 4,000 slaves clad in silken dress like those of the Caliph and on his death in 380/920 he left behind cash and property worth 40,000,000 *dinars* as his savings.[3] Wazīr Afdal possessed 120,000,000 *dīnars* besides other valuables and 800 slave girls despite the fact that he was known for his justice and good morale and according to Muyassar he never deprived anybody of his property.[4] 'Abdah, a daughter of Mu'izz, left behind after her death in 442/1050-51 five bags of precious stones and hundred boxes containing 3,000 silver utensils besides other valuables. The sister of Hākim namely Sitt al-Mulk was also known for living a luxurious life having 800 slave girls and an earning of 50,000 *dīnars* a year, This speaks of the abundance of wealth possessed by the Fatimids and hence the prosperity enjoyed by the upper class in the country.

Public works:—In Egypt the Nile played a very important role in irrigation as well as in navigation. The same irrigation system worked in Egypt as it did in 'Irāq. The Nile connected the Egyptian metropolis, Cairo, with other important towns and ports on it. Having Farāmah on its mouth and 'Aydhab on the Red Sea opposit to its upper part the Nile was also used for carrying trade between the Mediterranean rigions and the Red Sea and Arabian Sea ports. This route was utilized mostly by the Syrian and Jewish merchants who carried on international trade with oriental and occidental wares.[5]

---

1. Ibn al-Sairfi, p. 92; Wustenfeld, p. 149
2. Lane-Poole, *Coins and Medals*, pp. 165-67
3. Zahid 'Ali, *Ta'rikh-i-Fatimi'in Misr*, II, 130-31; Maqrizi, III, 7-11, Lane-Poole, p. 121
4. *Ibid.*, 132
5. *Cf.* Ibn Khurdadbih, pp. 153-54

By opening a large canal at Alexandria from the estuary of the Nile into the Mediterranean Sea for irrigation and navigation purpose enabling big vessels to sail inland the *Qadi* of Egypt served the purpose of *Hisbah* under al-Mutawakkil.[1] The Caliph also got repaired the water conduits of Alexandria which enjoyed a prosperous agriculture and a flourishing commerce leading to the growth of population in Alexandria.[2]

Although there were many itineraries of the Nile in the medieval period (7th - 11th century) and the facts and figures of these are scattered in the medieval historical and geographical literatures, their comprehensive and systematic accounts are yet to be collated.[3] The Rosetta and Damietta branches were the two main arms of the Nile in the 12th century. They differed from their present course only at Shatanuf and Damirah respectively. The third itinerary of the Nile corresponding to the modern al-*Bahr al-Saghir* was Khalij Tinnis. Of the other itineraries of the Nile in the 12th century Khalij al-Iskandriyah and Khalij Shanasha have disappeared due to silting. Nahr Abi al-Munajja the chief of the southern canals was constructed in 506/1113.[4] Another great canal Nahr Muwais, the so-called *Nahr Mu'izz*, of the Fatimid period is still extant. Khalij Miṣr which once united Fuṣṭāt with the Red Sea corresponds to the modern Isma'iliyah canal and reached as far as Birkat et Timsah in the 10th century.[5] About the 9th century Ibn Serapion recorded that Khalij Saradus irrigated *al-Sharqiyah* province upto Saradus a village in that of *al-Gharbiyah*[6] on the Nile at one day's journey both from Fustāt and Damietta until the construction of Nahr Abi al-Munajja. At its upper part the Khalij Saradus corresponded to the Damietta arm and at its lower part with Khalij Tinnis having another off shoot at a distance of thirty miles from the Nile and flowing both into the Mediterranean Sea between Damietta and Rosetta.[7]

---

1. *Wulat*, pp. 469-70
2. Severus, Vol. II, pt. I, p. 11 quoted by Shamsuddin Miah, p. 267n2
3. *Cf.* A. R. Guest, *The Delta (of the Nile) in the Middle Ages* in the *Journal of Royal Asiatic Society of Great Britain and Ireland*, London, 1912, pp. 942-44
4. Maqrizi, *Khitat*, I, 487:
5. Ma'sudi, *Muruj al-Dhahab*, I, p. 147
6. *Khitat*, I, 487
7. *The Delta in the Middle Ages*, A note on the branches of the Nile and the Kurahs of Lower Egypt by A. R. Guest in the *Journal of Royal Asiatic Society of Great Britain and Ireland*, London, 1912, p. 944

With the elaborate irrigation works, many swampy regions in the Lower Egypt were reclaimed, dry lands were irrigated and all-round economic development was witnessed during the Abbasid and Fatimid periods. With the economic change corresponding changes were brought in the social structure and urban development.

The plan of the city of Cairo was drawn by Caliph Mu'izz himself at his capital Mansuriyah near Qairawan in North Africa and was executed by his general Jawhar the conqueror of Egypt. On Saturday 24th Jumadi al-Awwal 359/March 970 the foundation of *al-Qahirah* city (Cairo) was laid by Jawhar between Mount Muqattam and the Bay to the north of Fustat by constructing two palaces for Abu Tamim Ma'ad al-Mu'izz namely *Qasr Kabīr* and *Qasr Saghir* leaving a parade ground for 10,000 soldiers in between the two palaces and was completed in two and a half years, the period of a severe famine in Egypt. Various *Diwan Khanahs* and *Aiwans* were constructed in these two palaces. Mu'izz, leaving his capital Mansuriyah on the 6th of August 972 and handing over North Africa to his vassal Bulugin b. Ziri, a Sanhajah Berber Chief, entered into Cairo through the Bab al-Zawilah in Sha'ban 362/May 972-3. The city went on developing until Salahuddin constructed a fort and allowed commoners to construct their houses in the southern and western suburbs of Cairo encircling Cairo and Fustat. Jawhar who was known for the construction of the *Jami'al-Azhar* at the behest of 'Aziz further constructed a *madrasah* and a library within the mosque. For about 200 years it functioned as a *Shi'i* institution and students from Turkey, India, Yaman, Zanjibar and al-Maghrib flocked on there to reeeive free religious and secular education.[1]

Like the Mughal Emperor Shah Jahan of India, 'Aziz also patronised art and architecture. Among the palaces constructed during his time were *Qasr al-Dhahab* and *Qasr al-Bahr* and among the mosques, Mosque of Qarafah[2] and *Jami' Anwar* which also became known as Hakim's mosque as it was completed by him.

The college and library of *Daru'l 'Ilm* or *Daru'l Hikmah* founded on the Bay of Alexandria were widened besides the construction

1. Zahid 'Ali, I, p. 161-64. *Cf.* Wiet, Gaston, *Histoire de Egyptiene*, Tome IV *(L' Egypte Arabe)*, 187-8
2. Zahid 'Ali, I, p. 205

of a number of mosques endowed with monthly allowances.[1] Although Hākim was hard towards the Sunnis as he was to the Christians and the Jews he opened a *madrasah* for the study of Maliki theology as the Sunnis were always in majority in Egypt.[2]

Resume :—The 'Arab Muslims came from Arabia the land of desert and expanded their empire from Chinese Turkistan and the Indus valley in the East to the Atlantic coast in the West and from the Arabian Sea and the Saḥarah desert in the south to Central Asia, the Caspian Sea and the Rhone valley across the Pyrenees in the north covering West Asia, North Africa and south-west Europe, the better parts of the three continents. The Arabs adopted the manners and customs of the natives if not contrary to the Islamic teachings deduced from the *Qura'n* and *Hadith* and taught them their own religion, language and culture. They were the followers of Prophet Muḥammad (570-632) and were led by the dynamic personalities like Hadrat Abū Bakr and 'Umar b. al-Khattab from the pious caliphs (632-661), Mu'awiyah, 'Abdu'l Malik, Walid I and 'Umar II from the Umayyads (661-749), Abu Ja'far al-Manṣūr, Hārūn al-Rashīd and Ma'mūn al-Rashid from the Abbasids (750-1258), 'Abd al-Raḥmān al-Dākhil, Hakam I, 'Abd al-Raḥmān al-Awsat, 'Abd al-Raḥman al-Nāṣir and Hakam II from the Umayyads of Spain (711-1031) and Mahdī, Mu'izz, 'Aziz and al-Hākim from the Fatimids of Egypt (909-1171).

These caliphs were assisted in the expansion and consolidation of the empire by brave generals and wise governors like Khalid b. Walīd, 'Amr b. al-'Aṣ, Abū 'Ubaydah, Sa'ad b. Abi Waqqāṣ, Hajjāj b. Yūsuf, Naṣr b. Sayyār, Mūsā b. Nuṣayr, Tāriq b. Zayyad, 'Abd al-Raḥmān b. Muslim, Yaḥyā b. Khālid al-Barmaki, Niẓām al-Mulk, Ibn Tūlūn, al-Jawhar, Ya'qub ibn Killis and Hājib al-Manṣūr. They were the dignitaries of their time and contributed their best to the nourishment of administrative institutions. While tracing the history of the development of these institutions in this handy volume references have been made to the services rendered by these personalities and to the impact of the Byzantine and Persian administration on Muslim administrative institutions and also

1. Zahid 'Ali, I, 243-47
2. *Ibid.*, II, p. 97. This is a revised edition, of the paper publishd in the *Journal of Asiatic Society of Pakistan*, XIV 1969, 256-269 no. 3, pp.

attempts have been made to discuss their political, social and economic impact on the urban and country life of the *Arabs*, *Mawalis* and *Dhimmis*.

Islam was not merely a religious faith but was indeed a way of life embracing, as it did within it, fully-developed political and administrative machineries of state, based as they were firstly on religious, social and economic foundations. Prophet Muḥammad was that rare phenomenon: both a leader of society and state. The Charter of Madinah, the Truce of Hudaybiyah and the Fare well Sermon that he delivered on the occasion of his last pilgrimage to Ka'abah are some of the proofs of his genius as a statesman.

The establishment of 'Umar's *Dīwan* (Finance Department) was the first attempt made in the history of the world by a state to take upon itself the collective responsibility for supplying food and clothing to the entire population. The Umayyads' contribution to the politico-social, economic and literary fields was remarkable. Mu'awiyah had the credit of introducing two Persian institutions, *Dīwan al-Khatam* (Bureau of registry) and *Dīwan al-Barīd* (Postal service) and also of establishing the naval power for the first time in Islam. By maintaining Public register in Arabic and minting pure-Arabic coins, *dinar* and *dirham*, the work of Arabicization introduced by 'Umar I was completed by 'Abd al-Malik. By revising weights and measures al-Walid brought about stability in rural life. In the expansion of administrative institutions, hospitals and caravanserais, mosques and educational institutions, and in the provision of irrigation and navigation, bathing and marketing facilities the services of the Abbasid Caliphs, especially Hārūn and Ma'mūn, were marvellous.

In the rise and fall of the Muslim dynasties there were discernible gleams of intellectual light. The Muslim rulers and savants have preserved the learning and culture of the ancient days by their patronage and in their writings. The Abbasid period is particularly known for the advancement of literature and science and within a century the Muslims had acquired admirable scientific knowledge through the Indian, Persian and Greek sources. The Magians converted to Islam brought the Indian and Persian influence in Arabic literature, science and philosophy. The literary sphere remained a virgin field for the Sanskrit and Persian influence as Greek drama, poetry and history were not translated into Arabic. The Muslims came into contact w Greek culture at Alexandria and in the Syrian and Mesopotamian towns through Aramaic and Syriac languages. The remnants of Babylionism, Indus Valley and Nile Valley civilizations received nourishment in the cradle of Islam.

Among the works on administration and political science the *Kitab al-Kharaj* of Qādī Abū Yūsuf (d. ca. 798), *Kitab al-Ahkam al-Sultaniyah* of al-Māwardi (d. 1058), *Siyasat Namah* of Niẓam al-Mulk (d. 1091 A.C.) and *Muqaddamah* to *Kitab al-'Ibar* of Ibn Khaldūn (d. March 1406) are worth mentioning. The other fields in which the Muslims made considerable progress were astronomy, mathematics, cartography, surgery, medicine, optics and philosophy. The Christian and Jewish scholars of Medieval Europe were very much indebted to them and read their works in Latin translations for centuries. Among such works mention may be made of *Sind Hind* of al-Fazari, the *Zijj* of al-Khawarizmi, *Ilkhani tables* of Nāṣir al-Din Tusi (d. 1274) and the *Zijj al-Kabir* of 'Ali ibn Yūnus (d. 1009) on astronomy, the *Algebra* of al-Khwarizmi on mathematics, the *Firdausu'l Hikmah* of 'Ali b. Rabban al-Tabari, *al-Hawi* of Abū Bakr Muḥammad al-Rāzī (Rhazes d. 925), *Qanūn fi al-Tib* (Canon of Medicine) of Abu 'Ali Husain ibn Sina (Avicenna d.1037), *al-Judari wa'l Hasbah* of Razi and the *Kitab al-Manazirah* of Alhazen ('Ali al-Hasan ibn al-Haytham d. 538/1090) on medical science and the works of al-Farabi, Ibn Sina (Avicenna) and Ibn Rushd (Averroes) on philosophy. Through their Latin translations the 'Arab science and the Greek philosophy of Platonism and Aristotelianism found their way into Europe. By writing *Risalah fi Ara' Ahl al-Madinah al-Fadilah* and *al-Siyasah* (*Siyasat*) *al-Madaniyah* in the line of Plato's *Republic* and Aristotle's *Politics*, al-Farabi won the title of *al-Mu'allim al-Thani* (the second teacher), the first being Great Stagirite. Ghazzāli's works *Ahya 'Ulum al-Din, Fatihat al-'Ulum* and *Tahafut al-Falasifah* reconciled Muslim theology with Greek philosophy and modified orthodoxy. Ghazzali's attack on rationalism was refuted in the *Tahafut al-Tahafat al-Falasifah* by the Spanish Muslim philosopher Ibn Rushd whose Commentaries on Aristotle creatad agitation in Europe.

BIBLIOGRAPHY

'Abbās Hamdānī — *The Fatimids*, Karachī, 1962

'Abd al-'Azīz al-Dūrī — *Ta'rīkh al-'Iraq al-Iqtasadī fi'l Qarn al-Rubā al-Hijri*, Baghdād 1367/1948.

Abū Dā'ud — *Kitab al-Kharaj*

Abu'l Farj al-Isf. — *Kitab al-Āghani*, Vol XV, Bulaq 1286H

Abu'l Fida — *Geografia*, I, III, Alger. 1839.

Alarcon — *Lampara de los Principes*, Vol. II, Mad. 1931.

Altamira — *Historia de Espana y de la civilisacion espanola*, Barcelona, 1911.

Amari, M. — *Storia dei Musulmani de Sicilia*, III, Cat. 1937-9

Al-Andalus, Vol. II, Madrid—Granada

Anonymous — *Akhbar Majmū'ah Cronica anonima del siglo* XI or *Majmu'ah-i-Akhbar Andalus* ed. by E. Lafuente y Alcantara, Madrid, 1867.

Arnold, T.W. — *The Preachings of Islam*, London, 1913

— *The Caliphate*, Oxford, 1967

Atlidi — *I'lam al-Nas*, Cairo, 1297 A.H.

Al-Balādhurī — *al-Futūh al-Buldan* ed. by de Goeje, Leyden, 1869. Eng. tr. by P.K. Hitti, Newyork, 1916.

Bayhaqqī — *Ta'rīkh-i-Mas'ūdī*, Calcutta, 1862.

Bell, M. — *Administration of Egypt under the Umayyad Caliphate*, 1928.

Bury, J.B. — *A History of the Later Roman Empire*, Vol. II, London, 1912.

Cambridge Medieval History, Vol. III.

Al-Dabbī — *Bughyat al-Multamis fi Ta'rīkh Rijal ahl Andalus*, (BAH, III), Madrid, 1885.

Al-Dhahabī — *Tadhkirat al-Huffaz*, I-IV, Hyderabad, 1333.

De Goeje — *Fragmenta Historicorum Arabicorum*, Vol. I

Dozy, Reinhart — *Spanish Islam (A History of the Moslems in Spain)*, Enlg. tr. by Stokes, London, 1913.

Eclipse of the Abbasid Caliphate, 7 Vols ed. & tr. by H.E. Amedroz and D.S. Margoliouth, Oxford, 1920-1.

Encyclopaedia of Islam, I-IV.

Fahmy, Aly Mohammed —*Muslim Sea Power in the Eastern Mediterranean Sea*, London, 1950.

Al-Fakhrī, Muḥammad b. 'Alī —*Adab al-Sultaniyah wal-Dual al-Islamiyah*, Cairo, 1899.

Gayangos, Pascual de —*The History of the Muhammadan Dynasties*. Engl. tr. of Maqqari's *Nafḥ al-Tib*, London, 1840-43.

Gomez, Emilio Garcia —*El Tratado de Ibn 'Abdūn* (Sp. tr. of Ibn 'Abdun's *al-Hisbah*).

—*Historia de Espana*, IV, (Sp. tr. of Levi-Provencal's *Histoire*), Madrid, 1958.

—*Eulogio del Islam Espanol* (al-Shaqundī), Madrid, 1954.

Gottheil, Richard —*Dhimmis and Muslims in Egypt*, Chicago 1908.

—*A distinguished family of Fatimid Qadis in the Tenth Century* in *the Journal of the American Oriental Society*, XXIX, 1909.

Ham'dullah, M. —*Rasūl-i-Akram Kī Siyasī Zindagī*. Karachi, '61.

Hamiltan and Grady —*Hidayah*, A commentary on the Muhammadan Law, London, 1870.

Harris, M. —*Egypt under the Egytians*, London, 1925.

Hasan, A. I —*Miṣr fi'l-'Uṣur al-Wustah*, Cairo, 1947.

—*Al-Fatimiyun fi Miṣri*, Cairo, 1932.

Hilāl al-Sābī —*Tuḥfatu'l Umara' bi Ta'rīkh al-Wuzara*, Beirut, 1904.

Himyarī —*Kitab al-Rawdat al-Mi'tar* ed. Levi-Provencal, Leiden, 1938.

Hitti, P. K. —*History of the Arabs*, London, 1951.

Hole, Edwyn —*Andalus: Spain under the Muslims*, London, '58.,

Husainī, S.A.Q. —*Arab Administration*, Lahore, 1957.

Ibn al-'Abbās —*Athar al-Uwal fi Tartib al-Duwab*, Cairo, 1295

Ibn Athīr —*Usd al-Ghabah fi Ma'rifat al Saḥabah*, Vol. VI, Cairo, 1826 A.H.

—*Al-Kamil fi al-Ta'rīkh*, 12 Vols. Cairo, 1274H

Ibn Bashkuwāl —*Kitab al-Silah* ed. by Codera, 2 Vols. Mad. '83.

Ibn Bassām —*Dhakhirah fi Maḥasin al-Jazīrah*, Vol. I/II, IV/I, Cairo, 1939-1945.

Ibn al-Faqih	—*Kitab al-Buldan*, ed. De Goeje, Leyden, 1302 H
Ibn al-Faradī	—*Kitab Ta'rīkh 'Ulama' al-Andalus* (BAH, III), Madrid, 1890-91. A. C.
Ibn al-Furat	—*Nishwar al-Muhadarah.*
Ibn Hammād	—*Akhbar al-Mulūk bani 'Ubayd wa Siratihim*, Paris, 1927 (tr. by M. Vonderheyden, text relating to the History of North Africa).
Ibn Hawqal	—*Manaqib Baghdad.*
	—*Al-Masalik wa'l Mamalik*, Leyden, 1938, (Ibn Hawqal's *Sūrat al-Ard*).
Ibn Hishām	—*Sirat al-Rasul Allah*, 2 Vols. ed. Wustenfeld, Gottingen, 1858.
Ibn 'Idhārī al-Marrākushī	—*Al-Bayan al-Maghrib fi Akhbar al-Maghrib*, Leiden, 1851, III, Paris, 1930.
	—*Azhar al-Riyad fi Akhbar 'Iyad*, 2 vols. Cairo, 1357/1940.
Ibn Ishāq	—*Sirat Rasul Allah*, A. Guillaume, Oxford, 1955.
Ibn al-Jawzī	—*Sirat 'Umar ibn 'Abd al-'Azīz*, Cairo, 1331H.
Ibn Jubayr	—*Rihlah*, ed. Wright de Goeje, Leyden, 1907.
	—*Rihlat Ibn Jubair* by Gibb.
Ibn Khaldūn	—*Al-Muqaddamah*, Fr. tr. *Prolegomenes* by de Slane, Paris, 1925-7.
	—*Kitab al-'Ibar*, 7 vols. Cairo, 1284/1868.
Ibn Khallikān	—*Wafiyat al-A'yan*, 3 vols., Cairo, 1310.
	—*Biographical Dictionary*, Fr. tr. by de Slane 4 Vols. Paris, 1842-71.
Ibn al-Khatib	—*Kitab A'mal al-A'lam*, ed. by Lovi-Provencal, Rabat, 1353/1934.
Ibn Khurdādbih	—*Al-Masalik wa'l Mamalik*, Leyden, 1889.
Ibn Qutaybah	—*'Uyunu'l-akhbar*, 4 vols. Cairo, 1925-30, ed. Brockelmann, Berlin, 1900-08
Ibn al-Qūtiyah	—*Ta'rīkh Iftitah al-Andalus* Madrid, 1868, ed. and tr. by Ribera, *J. Historia de la Conquista de Espana, Madrid, 1926.*
Ibn Rustah	—*al-A'laq al-Nafisah*, 1891.
Ibn Sa'd	—*Kitab al-Tabaqat al-Kabīr*, 9 vols. ed. E. Sachau Leyden, 1905/1940
Ibn Tabtaba	—*Ta'rīkh al-Rusūl wa'l Mulūk*, 11 vols. Cairo, 1326.
Ibn Taghribardi, A.M.	—*Al-Nujūm al-Zahirah fi Mulūk Misr wa'l Qahirah*. 5 vols. California, 1909-29. Cairo, '33.

Ibn al-Tiqtaqā —*Al-Fakhrī*, ed. W. Ahlwardt, Gotha, 1860.
— " ed. H. Derenbourg, Paris, 1895.

Al-Idrīsī —*Dhikr al-Andalus* (extracts from *Nuzhat al-Mushtaq*) ed. and tr. by A. Conde, Madrid, 1890

Imamuddin, S.M.—*A Political History of Muslim Spain* (Revised and enlarged edition), Karachi, 1974.

—*Some Aspects of the Socio-Economic and Cultural History of Muslim Spain*, Leiden, 1965.

—*A Political History of the Muslims*, Vol. I (*Prophet and Pious Caliphs*), Dacca, 1965. Vol. II (*Umayyads and Abbasids*), Dacca, 1972.

—*Economic History of Spain under the Umayyads*, Dacca, 1965

—*Administration under the Fatimids* in *the Journal of Asiatic Society of Pakistan*, Dacca, 1969.

Islamic Culture, Hyderabad (Deccan, India), 1958-1960.

Al-Iṣṭakhrī —*The Kitab Masalik al-Mamalik* (BGA, Vol. I), Madrid, 1870.

Ivanow, W. —*The Rise of the Fatimids*, Oxford, 1942.

Al-Jahshiyari —*Kitab al-Wuzara' wa'l Kuttab*, Cairo, 1938, Leipzig, 1926.

Joseph Hell —*The Arab Civilization*, Eng. tr. by S. Khuda Bakhsh, Lahore, 1943.

Journal of Royal Asiatic Society, London, 1912, 1930.

Jurjī Zaydān —*Ta'rīkh Tamaddun-i-Islamī* (Urdu tr. by Muḥammad Halim Anṣārī), 2 vols. Karachi, 1960, Arabic text, Egypt, 1902-22.

—*Umayyads and Abbasids*, tr. D S. Margoliouth, Leyden, 1907.

Juwayni —*Ta'rīkh-i-Jahan Kusha'i* ed. Muḥammad Qazwīnī, 3 vols. London and Leyden, 1912-37.

Kalib Chalibi, M.—*Kashf al-Zunūn*.

Kanz al-'Ummal fi Sunani'l Aqwal, 8 vols. Cairo, 1312 A.H.

Khuda Bakhsh —*Renaissance of Islam*, Patna, 1937.

—*Orient under the Caliphs*, Calcutta, 1920.

—*Islamic Civilization*, 2 vols. Calcutta, 1930.

Al-Khudari —*Ta'rīkh Umami'l Islamiyah*, 3 vols. Cairo, 1934

Al-Khushanī al-Qarawi —*Kitab al-Qudat* ed. & tr. by J. Ribera, Madrid, 1914.

Al-Kindī —*Kitab al-Wulat wa'l-Qudat*, ed. by Rhuven Guest, London, 1912.

Lammens, N. —*La Syrie : precis historique*, Beirut, 1921.

Lane-Poole, Stanley —*A History of Egypt in the Middle Ages*, London 1901.

—*Coins and Medals.*

Le Strange —*The Lands of the Eastern Caliphate*, Cambridge, 1930

Levy, Reuben —*The Social Structure of Islam* (*An Introduction to the Sociology of Islam)*, Cambridge, 1957.

Levy-Provencal —*Histoire de L'Espagne Musulmans*, 3 vols. Paris, 1950.

—*L'Espagne Musulman*, au X siecle, Paris, 1932.

Lopez de Ayala —*Contribuciones e impuestos en Leon Y Castilla durante la Edad Media*, Madrid, 1898.

Ma'alim al-Qurbah fi aḥkam al-Hisbah (Gibb XII), London, 1938.

Mālik b. Anas —*Al-Muwattah*, Cairo, 1280 H.

McCabe, Joseph —*Splendour of Moorish Spain*, London, 1935.

Al-Maqqarī —*Nafh al-Tib min G̲h̲usn al-Andalus al-Ratib*, I-X, Cairo, 1949, Engl. tr. by Gayangos, Pascual de, *The History of the Muhammadan dynasties in Spain*, London, 1940-43.

—*Azhar al-Riyad fi al-Akh̲bar*, *Iyad*, Cairo, 1357/1940.

Al-Maqrīzī —*K̲h̲itat al-Miṣr*, 2 vols. Bulaq (Egypt), 1270H.

—*Histoire des Sultans Mamlouks del Egypte*, tr. Quatremere, Paris, 1837-62

—*Itti'az al-Hunafa*, ed. Shayyal, Cairo, 1948.

Al-Mas'ūdī —*Murūj al-D̲h̲ahab*, ed. and tr. Barbier de Meynard and Pavet de Courteille, 9 vols. Paris

Al-Māwardī, A.H—*Al-Aḥkam al-Sultaniyah*, Cairo, 1909, ed. M. Enger, Bonn, 1853.

Mez, A. —*El Renacimiento del Islam* (Sp. tr. by Salvador Vila), Madrid, 1936.

—*The Renaissance of Islam* (Engl. tr. by K̲h̲uda Bak̲h̲s̲h̲ and Margoliouth, London, 1937.

Miskawayh —*The Eclipse of the Abbasid Caliphate*, ed. & tr. Amedroz, 7 vols. Oxford, 1920-21.

Al-Mubarrad —*Al-Kamil*, Cairo 1286H. ed. W. Wright, Leipzig, 1864.

Muḥammad Shamsuddin Miah —*The Reign of al-Mutawakkil*, ASB, Dacca, 1971.

Muir, William —*Annals of Early Caliphate*, London, 1883.

—***The Caliphate, Its Rise, Decline and Fall***, **Edinburgh, 1915.**

Musharrafa, 'Atiyah Mus'afa —*Nuzum al-Hukm bi Misr fi 'asr al-Fatimiyyin*, Cairo, 1919.

Musnad Ibn Hanbal, IV.

Nadvī, Shah Mu'in al-Dīn —*Ta'rīkh-i-Islam*, Part III (*Khilafat-i-'Abbasiyah*).

Nadvī, S. Sulaymān —*Arbon Kī Jahazranī*, Azamgarh, 1935.

—*'Arab Hind Ke Ta'llūqat.*

Nāsir Khusraw —*Safarnamah.*

Nicholson — *Literary History of the Arabs*, Cambridge, 1930.

Nizām al-Mulk —*Siyasat Namah*, C. Schefer, Paris, 1891-5.

Al-Nuwayrī —*The Kitab Nihayat al-Arab* ed. & Fr. tr. by Gaspar Y Remiro, Granada, 1917.

O'Leary, De Lacy —*A Short History of the Fatimid Caliphate*, Newyork, 1923

Poliak —*Feudalism in Egypt, Syria, Palestine and Lebanon.*

Al-Qalqashandī — *Subh al-A'sha*, III, Cairo, 1913.

Qudāmah - *Kitab al Kharaj*, Leyden, 1306 H.

Rhuven Guest —*The History of the Egyptian Qadis*, ed. Richard Gottheil, Paris, 1908.

Al-Sābī - *Kitabu'l-Wuzara'* ed. Amedroz, Leyden, 1904.

Sadeque, S. F. —*Baybars I of Egypt*, Dacca, 1956.

Sairfi, Ibn —*Ru'asa'ul Kitab fi al-Dawlat al-Fatmiyah*,

Scott, S.P. — *History of the Moors in Europe*, 3 vols, Philadelphia, 1904.

Shāh Mu'in al-Dīn Nadvī --*Ta'rīkh-i-Islam*. Part III, Khilafat-i-'Abbāsiyah vol. I.

Shahristānī —*Kitab al-Milal wa'l nihal*, Cairo, 1263, ed. W. Cureton, London, 1846.

Shibli Nu'mānī —*Al-Farūq*, 2 vols. Lakhnaw, 1919, Eng. tr. *Umar the Great*, 2 vols. Lahore, 1939, 1951.

Al-Mu'ayyad —*Sirat al-Mu'ayyad fi'l-Din Da'i al-Du'at*, ed. Kāmil Husayn, Cairo, 1949.

Stern, S.M. —*Fatimid Decrees, Original Documents from the Fatimid Chancery*, London, 1964.

Al-Sulī —*Akhbar al-Radi wa al-Muttaqi bi'llah.*

Al-Suyūtī —*Husn al-Muhadarah fi Misr wa'l Qahirah.*

Tabarī —Ta'rīkh, 2 vols. Cario, 1299

—Ta'rīkh *Rusūl wa'l Muluk*, Vols. I-VI, ed. de Goeje, Leiden, 1889-1901

Tanūkhī —*Nishwar al-Muḥadarah*, ed. D.S. Margoliouth, London, 1921.

Al-Tartūshī, A.B. —*Siraju'l* Mulūk, Cairo, 1311 A.H.

Al-'Umarī —*Al-Ba'rif bi al*-Mustalah *al.Sharif*, Cairo, 1312.

Von Kremer —*The Orient Under the Caliphs*, (Engl. tr. by Khuda Bakhsh, Calcutta, 1920.).

Vatikiotis, P.J. —*The Fatimid Theory of State*, Lahore, 1957.

Watt, A.M. —*Muhammad at Mecca*, Oxford, 1953.

—*Muhammad at Medina*, Oxford, 1956.

Watt, W. M. —*A History of Islamic Spain*, Edinburgh, 1965

Wellhausen —*Arab Kingdom and its Fall*, Calcutta, 1927.

Wiet, Gaston —*Histoire de L'nation Egyptienne*, Tome IV, (L' Egypte *Arabe de la Conqueti arabe a la Conqueti Ottomane*, (642-1517), Paris, 1937.

Yahyā ibn Adam—*Kitab al-Kharaj*, Cairo, 1347 H.

Ya'qūbī —*Kitab al-Buldan*, Leyden, 1885-92.

—*Ta'rikh* (*Historiae*) ed. Houtsma, M. Th., Leyden, 1883.

Yāqūt —*Mu'jam al-Buldan*, 6 Vols. Leipzig, 1866-70.

—*Irshad*, II.

Yūsuf, Abū —*Kitab al-Kharaj*, Bulaq, 1302 H.

Zāhid 'Alī —*Ta'rikh Fatimiyin Miṣr*, 2 Vols. Karachi, 1963.

Zaydān, Jurjī —*Ta'rikh-i-Tamaddun Islam*, Vols. I-IV, Egypt, 1902-22.

—*Ta'rikh Miṣr al-Hadith*.

INDEX

—: o :—

AUTHOR

Dr. S. M. Imamuddin was born in Monghyr (1924) and educated in Calcutta. He graduated from Islamia College (1941) and obtained his Master's degree (1943) and Doctorate degrees from Calcutta University (1951) and Madrid University (1956). During this period he enjoyed Calcutta University Post-Graduate Fellowship, R. G. Casey Research Fellowship and Spanish Government Scholarship, visited monuments and museums and worked in the libraries of India, Spain, Spanish Morocco, England and France and taught Graduate and Post-Graduate students at Central Calcutta (Islamia) College, Calcutta University, India and Dacca University, Bangladesh

The Author has made researches on Moors' Rule in Spain and Afghans' rule in India and published nine text books and reference works in 13 volumes, four being on Muslim Spain alone, as enumerated elsewhere and also more than fifty research papers, about thirty being again on Muslim Spain in International Journals like *Al-Andalus*, *Islamic Culture*, *Islamic Studies*, *Dacca University Studies* and *Journal of Asiatic Society of Pakistan* and *Pakistan Historical Society*. His books have been reviewed in and outside Pakistan and in various European languages. His works were highly commended by scholars like Professor Hardy, Nevill Barbour, H. K. Sherwani and others. By writing books and papers on Spain he has made rich Spanish Muslim culture known to the English knowing world and established its great impact on other European cultures.

NAJMAHSONS, B-724/13, Federal 'B' Area
Karachi-38, Telephone - 680285